Praise for *Designed to Learn*

It's critically important for Portnoy's argument to get heard at every level—citizens, teachers, and schools of education. She proposes an excitingly different paradigm for meeting the challenge. I'm hoping soon to see my colleagues put it into action!

—**Deborah Meier,**
MacArthur award–winning educator, reformer, and author

A timely resource that needs to be in every teacher and administrator's hands. Lindsay Portnoy has provided us with the ultimate resource for transforming a school's curriculum. This book will fundamentally change your mindset and begs the reader to ask: Are we ready to share in the work of reviving purposeful education that encourages students to embrace their talents and maximize their fullest potential?

—**Michael J. Hynes,**
Superintendent of Schools for the Port Washington School District

Lindsay Portnoy is a force of nature: part teacher, part cognitive scientist, part instructional designer, part historian, part educational futurist. She is the perfect guide to help our schools navigate this uncertain time. Her book is essential reading.

—**Greg Toppo,**
author, *The Game Believes in You:*
How Digital Play Can Make Our Kids Smarter

DESIGNED TO LEARN

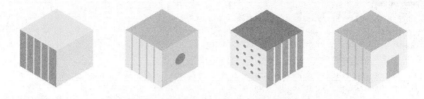

USING DESIGN THINKING

DESIGNED

TO BRING PURPOSE AND PASSION

TO LEARN

TO THE CLASSROOM

LINDSAY PORTNOY

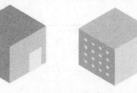

ASCD

Alexandria, Virginia USA

1703 N. Beauregard St. • Alexandria, VA 22311-1714 USA
Phone: 800-933-2723 or 703-578-9600 • Fax: 703-575-5400
Website: www.ascd.org • E-mail: member@ascd.org
Author guidelines: www.ascd.org/write

Ronn Nozoe, *Interim CEO and Executive Director;* Stefani Roth, *Publisher;* Genny Ostertag, *Director, Content Acquisitions;* Susan Hills, *Senior Acquisitions Editor;* Julie Houtz, *Director, Book Editing & Production;* Liz Wegner, *Editor;* Judi Connelly, *Senior Art Director;* Georgia Park, *Senior Graphic Designer;* Valerie Younkin, *Senior Production Designer;* Kelly Marshall, *Interim Manager, Production Services;* Shajuan Martin, *E-Publishing Specialist;* Tristan Coffelt, *Senior Production Specialist*

All web links in this book are correct as of the publication date below but may have become inactive or otherwise modified since that time. If you notice a deactivated or changed link, please e-mail books@ascd.org with the words "Link Update" in the subject line. In your message, please specify the web link, the book title, and the page number on which the link appears.

PAPERBACK ISBN: 978-1-4166-2824-8   ASCD product #120026

PDF E-BOOK ISBN: 978-1-4166-2826-2; see Books in Print for other formats.

Quantity discounts are available: e-mail programteam@ascd.org or call 800-933-2723, ext. 5773, or 703-575-5773. For desk copies, go to www.ascd.org/deskcopy.

ASCD Member Book No. FY20-2 (Nov. 2019 PSI+). ASCD Member Books mail to Premium (P), Select (S), and Institutional Plus (I+) members on this schedule: Jan, PSI+; Feb, P; Apr, PSI+; May, P; Jul, PSI+; Aug, P; Sep, PSI+; Nov, PSI+; Dec, P. For current details on membership, see www.ascd.org/membership.

Library of Congress Cataloging-in-Publication Data
Names: Portnoy, Lindsay, author.
Title: Designed to learn : using design thinking to bring purpose and passion to the classroom / Lindsay Portnoy.
Description: Alexandria, VA : ASCD, [2020] | Includes bibliographical references and index.
Identifiers: LCCN 2019026768 | ISBN 9781416628248 (paperback) | ISBN 9781416628262 (pdf)
Subjects: LCSH: Classroom environment. | Curriculum planning. | Student-centered learning.
Classification: LCC LB3013 .P6386 2020 | DDC 371.102/4--dc23
LC record available at https://lccn.loc.gov/2019026768

29 28 27 26 25 24 23 22 21 20   1 2 3 4 5 6 7 8 9 10 11 12

To my best teachers, Judah and Levi.
May you always use your voice for good and work
to design a more just and equitable future for all of us.

USING DESIGN THINKING TO BRING

DESIGNED TO LEARN

PURPOSE AND PASSION TO THE CLASSROOM

Introduction

Did you know when you wonder you're learning?

Fred Rogers

This story starts with Tech Valley, a dynamic high school in Albany, New York, that leverages community relationships to enhance student learning and help students see themselves as valuable members of their community who can bring about positive change. School outreach coordinator Sarah Fiess works tirelessly to bring in community members to share their expertise and demonstrate how students' classroom learning applies to the world outside school.

It was a week after one such visit that environmental science teacher Ashley Phillips introduced the topic of population dynamics. Using passages from Michael Pollan's book, *The Omnivore's Dilemma*, Phillips asked students to share their thoughts on food scarcity and its impact on the local and global community.

What followed was a sort of Socratic seminar in which students questioned human nutritional requirements, types of agriculture, genetic engineering, irrigation, and pesticides. One student recalled how a local information security expert who had visited the school made the connection between food scarcity and protecting resources against a cyberattack. Another student wondered aloud, "How can we help all people see the impact of the decisions they make on everyone in their community and our world?"

Phillips challenged the students to create an experience that would help people understand population dynamics. One student suggested creating a card game, a suggestion that was enthusiastically embraced. The game, ultimately named Pressing Issues, would include a series of cards that introduced a problem in the form of a question such as, "What are the best national policies that can be put in place to address overpopulation?" Players were to choose a solution from among the solution cards in their hands and then defend it. To create the game, students had to research the implications of population growth and enumerate the advantages and disadvantages associated with each of the myriad solutions. To refine and improve the game, they solicited feedback from peers who served as game testers.

And that's how a simple wondering turned into an amazing learning experience. As a guide on the side, the teacher was able to teach environmental science content in a way that was deeply engaging and driven by student learners.

Designing to Learn

Herein lies the promise of experiential learning—through the elements of *design thinking*. Design thinking entails creating learning environments that foster students' ability to design solutions to today's pressing problems. As in the example above, the process of *understanding* through *empathy* enabled learners to *identify* and *research* a specific problem to solve. Through *ideation*, learners worked collaboratively to identify a way to *communicate* their knowledge, in this case through the creation of an experience called Pressing Issues. Building a *prototype* of their game and *testing* it helped them improve their work. Through *iteration* and *reflection*, learners were able to identify the ways their understanding could influence their learning both today and in the future.

Teachers are the ultimate design thinkers. Every day, teachers enter classrooms to embark on the human-centered act of guiding our youngest citizens along their pathways to success. But the role of educator nearly always extends beyond the walls of the classroom to impact the broader communities we serve, traveling with each of our learners who carry a piece of our shared journey as they make their way in the world. Nowhere is student voice more influential than in a classroom of experiential learners using the lens of design thinking to solve problems in their world and work together to create a more sustainable future.

Why We Need It

By the year 2026, the rote tasks inherent in our current professions will be automated by technology, effectively changing or eliminating nearly two million jobs in the United States alone. Although these figures are typically used to incite fear, the reality is far more promising. According to the consulting firm McKinsey Global Institute, by 2030 there will be a surge of over 200 million new careers (Manyika et al., 2017). These new roles will no longer ask learners to simply collect and process data but, instead, to apply expertise, interact with stakeholders, and navigate complex relationships. Students will be called on to use their uniquely human skills of collaboration, communication, empathy, and divergent thinking as they move into an uncertain but exciting future. The process of design thinking as described in this book naturally hones these skills by engaging learners in meaningful work.

A Look at the Book

Designed to Learn is divided into two parts. The first section looks at design thinking globally. It begins with a research-based overview of the five elements of design thinking and provides methods for formatively assessing learning at each step. In Chapter 1, we see how design thinking encourages students to take perspective and empathize with others in their classroom and in the wider community. As they identify problems, students learn to work effectively with others, listen to varying perspectives, and support their thinking with evidence.

Design thinking necessarily shifts the roles of educators and students in the classroom. Chapter 2 unpacks those roles and details how student inquiry and developmentally appropriate content enable educators to provide multiple ways of solving problems across the curriculum. Chapter 3 examines how a few simple shifts in planning can transform traditional instruction into purposeful, multimodal, engaged learning. Design thinking drives student engagement by giving learners the *why* behind learning content through active application and inquiry.

The process of design thinking begins when students use their content knowledge to identify a meaningful problem to solve and then work together to create solutions. We'll address these issues in the second part of the book, each chapter of which will tackle one of the five elements in design thinking. In Chapter 4, we'll see how students tackle the first element, *understand and empathize.* Here they learn how to take on new perspectives to build empathy for others while broadening their view of the world around them. In science classes, they may study how new buildings in their town affect the local water supply. In social studies, they may uncover the history of a local law and wish to learn more about its impact on their community.

Understanding for empathy supports learners in identifying opportunities for designing innovations, but how do students know if the problem they've identified is a mere symptom or the root cause? Chapter 5 focuses on the second element in the process, *identify and research.* Here we'll discuss why guiding students in identifying the root cause of a problem is one of the most complex aspects of design thinking and a valuable opportunity for fostering future-ready learners.

During the ideation phase of the process, students draw from their cross-curricular understanding to put forth innovative solutions to a problem. Scaffolding ideation in the classroom requires careful listening and critical feedback. Chapter 6 deals with the third element in the design thinking process, *communicate to ideate.* It provides concrete methods for supporting students in evaluating the feasibility and impact of designs while engaging in effective communication to advocate for change.

Having identified a need and ideated solutions, students must now carefully select, build, and test the prototype they believe is most promising. Chapter 7 considers the fourth element, *prototype and test.* It offers concrete strategies for evaluating student work, as well as vignettes demonstrating how students can prototype and test designs across the curriculum.

Once students have created and tested their prototype, they must carefully evaluate the feedback to determine how well their solution addressed the identified problem. Chapter 8 focuses on the last element in the design thinking process, *iterate and reflect.* It suggests multiple ways for teachers to support students in categorizing feedback that either supports or rejects their designed solution in ways that foster empathy, develop clear communication skills, and support collaboration toward a shared goal. This chapter concludes the description of the key components of the design thinking process.

Each chapter of the book emphasizes the crucial importance of ongoing feedback in making learning visible and ensuring that learners take the lead in their own learning. You'll find student self-assessments and peer assessments. You'll find questions for both teachers and students in each of the five elements that get at the heart of learning. And you'll find a plethora of tools that students can use to clarify their thinking, monitor their progress, and become successful designers and problem solvers.

In Notes from the Field, a section I've included at the end of each chapter, I offer case studies from teachers across the United States who use design thinking across the curriculum and across various levels of instruction. These teachers share the aspects of design thinking that have been the most challenging, most exciting, and most inspiring in their communities.

A Sneak Peek: Design Thinking in Action

In a 4th and 5th grade self-contained classroom at a large Title 1 school in Brooklyn, New York, the students weren't sure what to expect when teaching artists Jody Drezner Alperin and Vicky Finney Crouch from the educational organization Off the Page arrived in their classroom. The unit of study they would cover together included immigration; it spanned the same objectives covered across New York City public schools, including industrial growth and immigration during the early 1900s.

The typical instruction around immigration begins by sharing informational texts with the students in this 12:1 classroom. Together, teachers and students discuss how the lives of immigrants changed as they adapted to life in New York City. The readings and conversations typically culminate in a written essay or report. These are the traditional outcomes of this standard unit of study. But the teaching artists at Off the Page had a different idea.

In addition to some of the traditional readings, Drezner Alperin and Finney Crouch created simulations in which students experienced the lives of immigrants during the Industrial Revolution. From sorting buttons in a factory to navigating a system in a new language, learners quickly connected the experiences of the past with those of the present. Most of the children in the class, themselves immigrants, readily identified with the experiences of those children from over a century ago. What's more, several children offered, "In my country, kids still work."

Understanding immigration during the Industrial Revolution and empathizing with new immigrants took on a deeper meaning as students began to research current practices in countries around the world. Students learned that although the United States long ago banned child labor, many of the countries from which students hailed still allowed such practices to continue. Learners wondered how they could help raise awareness of this issue across their community. In researching the problem further, students realized that many of the goods purchased locally come from places where child labor continues. What's more, learners discovered a free mobile app that enables users to discover the country of origin of many of the products they purchase.

Students brainstormed a list of ways they could raise awareness of this issue. They decided to create a campaign to inform the entire community about how to download the free mobile app so community members would know more about the products they were purchasing. The community embraced this tool and became far more mindful of where their purchases were produced.

This design thinking experience met the same requirements as typical instruction about immigration during the height of the Industrial Revolution, but it yielded significantly deeper outcomes, including more engaged learners and an empowered community. Through empathizing, defining the problem, ideating, prototyping, and testing the impact of their campaign, students began to see themselves as more than simply receivers of knowledge; they saw themselves as transmitters of hope and power in building a more just future.

Are You Ready?

You, too, can transform your curriculum into an invitation for innovation with minimal effort and maximum reward. In the pages that follow, I'll equip you with the necessary strategies and supports to do so. The question now is this: Are you ready to share in the work of reviving purposeful education that encourages students to embrace their uniquely human skills as they prepare for future roles that are as yet undefined?

1
...

Finding Purpose in Learning

We do not need magic to change the world, we carry all the power we need inside ourselves already: We have the power to imagine better.

J. K. Rowling

Think about the last time you learned something new. Did you pick up a non-fiction book about deep space to pursue your latent passion for understanding life beyond our atmosphere? Perhaps you taught yourself to knit as part of a community effort to send blankets to those left devastated after a natural disaster. Maybe you decided to take a crack at crafting your own artisanal brews at home.

What prompted you to engage in this new learning? The *why* is the impetus that drove you to learn to speak a new language, play an instrument, or code long after your days as a student. This drive fuels your sense of purpose and passion, according to researcher Dan Pink (2011); it motivates you to engage your innate curiosity in the pursuit and application of new knowledge. Creative learning strategist Barbara Bray (2015) suggests that "defining your why" may very well be the key to unlocking your true potential in learning and life.

Now think about *how* you approached learning that something new, or, more specifically:

- If you got stuck, where did you seek support?
  - How did you identify sources for research?
  - What were the attributes of those sources that rendered them reliable?

- How did you know when you understood a concept?
  — For example, how did you distinguish between concepts like a purl and a knit stitch? How did you identify how much yeast to pitch in the fermenter?
  — When were you able to communicate your understanding to your friend, partner, or child?

- At what point were you ready to move beyond learning to doing?

As you learn and apply new knowledge that is meaningful to your life, you're already enacting elements of design thinking. The goal of this book is to act as a primer as you set the stage for design thinking in your classroom by providing simple strategies and clear tools to scaffold the iterative processes of inquiry, discovery, design, and reflection.

The elements of design thinking presented here invite students into the flexible process of learning and creating together, with you as their guide. Throughout each element, you'll see how to create more dynamic assessments that demonstrate and inform student learning. By doing so, you'll share some of the responsibility of assessment with your students to develop their self-regulation and metacognitive skills. Perhaps most important, you'll spend more time answering questions and less time in front of a classroom of students, their eyes glazed over.

Roll up your sleeves. It's about to get wonderfully messy.

Shifts That Have Paved the Way

Traditional education paradigms were initially modeled after needs for industrialization (i.e., factories, bells, siloed content), whereas needs for what Klaus Schwab (2016) has called the *fourth industrial revolution*—in which new technologies will fuse the physical, digital, and biological worlds on a grand scale—require interdisciplinary approaches to learning. Here, students are engaged in multimodal inquiry through holistic units of active learning and deep inquiry. Our education system isn't failing—it's changing.

Shifts in Pedagogy, Tools, and Content

Cultivating our youngest citizens to take on the important work of the future requires a shift in the way we teach them today. Teachers who are leading this change have adopted novel pedagogies, tools, and content to meet the needs of their students and set them on pathways to success.

Pedagogies. Foundational skills are necessary for success, but rote tasks have taken a back seat to instruction that cultivates deep and powerful learning driven by student curiosity. We're witnessing a shift in curriculum, spurred on by the need for students to synthesize important concepts; learning that was once a mile wide and an inch deep is giving way to learning that is a mile deep and an inch wide.

Measuring students' knowledge acquisition has also undergone a shift. Teachers scaffold formative assessments to drive student work forward; at the same time, formative feedback helps identify where students struggle and need support. When educators share the responsibility of assessment with their students, students become more self-reflective, independent learners who achieve greater agency and voice within the classroom.

Educators increasingly are encouraging student autonomy in problem solving. Students must demonstrate content knowledge in novel ways, given our deeper understanding of what it means, for example, to learn science. Digital and more traditional forms of learning and assessment support clearer communications between students and teachers because they enable educators to address students' questions as they arise, fostering more consistent growth and learning. Digital tools also enable educators to leverage their social networks to build, grow, and share their practice with a global community as they celebrate the diverse learning happening in our schools each day.

Tools. Technological advances offer novel affordances to engage learners and enable teachers to quickly collect feedback and pivot on instruction. Educators can get a baseline reading of student understanding and maximize class time by focusing on areas that need strengthening or on those that are innately interesting to learners. Alone, these are simply tools; in the hands of thoughtful educators, they become transformative.

For example, with a single smartphone and one piece of paper per student, teachers use tools like Plickers to conduct formative assessments. In classrooms that have gone one-to-one—that is, where every student has a computer or device—teachers collect feedback throughout instruction with tools like Nearpod or Socrative. What's more, those with access to smartphones and to Google Cardboard, a virtual reality platform, can now travel the globe and to the outer limits of the universe to experience what was once relegated to the pages of a textbook. These tools provide a template for rich experiences that enable students to talk with experts around the globe and that allow for dynamic feedback to drive inquiry.

Content. Students live rich lives outside the classroom; the design thinking process encourages them to bring this richness and variety into the classroom. As students grow foundational content knowledge (hard skills), they develop soft skills, such as working collaboratively in teams, taking the perspective of others, honing skills for solving complex problems, and demonstrating mindfulness. These skills help students feel connected to their classroom community and to the world at large. They also enable them to navigate the systems around them and find meaningful solutions to the pressing problems they encounter along the way.

Shifts in Cultural Tools

The cognitive theorist Lev Vygotsky (1978) once posited human learning as co-constructed within the specific social and cultural norms of the learner. The difference between what learners can do on their own and what they can accomplish with the help of a more knowledgeable other is what he referred to as their *zone of proximal development.* According to his research, a more knowledgeable other could scaffold student understanding to reach the upper limits of a student's zone through the use of cultural tools.

What Vygotsky might refer to as cultural tools—be they language or something more concrete, like an abacus or a calculator—are already changing the ways we engage with the world. Visionary educators who leverage new tools are curating content so their students receive relevant, timely, and developmentally appropriate information. When students see themselves as makers and creators of content, conversations arise about the multiple per-spectives embedded in each new literary passage, article, or chapter. These shifts have set the stage for pedagogies like design thinking to emerge, where educators and students work collaboratively and invite deeper inquiry for understanding.

The Science Behind Design Thinking

Before diving into an overview of the elements of design thinking, it's import-ant to note that student and teacher interests are central to purposeful learn-ing. A teacher is no longer "the sage on the stage" but rather "the guide on the side." This shift is key to fostering student autonomy and preparing stu-dents for the knowledge economy. We're born scientists, experimenting on the world around us to help us learn, change, and grow. The new tools we're bringing into the education system will automate the busywork that has monopolized teachers' time for so long and will free up educators to collabo-rate and innovate with their students.

A long history of learning science underlies the model of design thinking; it's rooted deep in constructivism, with nods from motivational research and various theories of learning. The teacher-led counterpart to design think-ing resides in the Understanding by Design® (UbD) framework (Wiggins & McTighe, 2011), which can be beneficial in getting you started with your first design thinking project. The UbD model guides teachers in developing cur-riculum by identifying the major learning outcomes students should demon-strate to show mastery. It then requires teachers to design backward to craft lessons that will scaffold instruction toward the learning goals.

Similar to teachers in a UbD context, teachers in design thinking class-rooms use standards-based content to determine the big ideas that stu-dents should understand during each unit. However, distinct from UbD and approaches like problem-based learning, design thinking puts the big ideas *first* by asking students to seek out and identify problems. It then works back-ward to identify information students must master as they design solutions that address problems or opportunities in the world around them.

As you'll read in subsequent chapters, while work toward the designed solutions unfolds, the learning outcomes become more than the sum of their parts. A unit on persuasive writing may transform into a multimedia social justice movement, or a unit on coding may culminate in a community-wide robot wedding. As students work to design solutions, the very nature of instruction and assessment shifts to incorporate related topics from across the curriculum in exciting and unforeseen ways.

Teachers in design thinking classrooms cultivate experiential learning that is standards based but student driven, distinct from transmission models of education (Richardson, 2005). Critics of constructivist learning suggest that student misconceptions are reinforced during student-led inquiry, yet the opposite is true in design thinking classrooms (Sewell, 2002). In these classrooms, students are called on to explain their understanding. Through iterative design and formative feedback, student understanding is made visible, and teachers can easily identify and address misconceptions.

As students begin to see how their designed solutions may affect the world around them, they learn through active inquiry alongside peers, educators, and members of their local and global community. This is the 21st century's version of a *cognitive apprenticeship* (Collins, Brown, & Newman, 1989), where giving students a sense of voice and agency in their learning helps them take on roles in their communities.

What emerges from the process is a sense of purpose that propels students forward as co-creators of knowledge (Pink, 2011). As students apply the knowledge and skills they've acquired, they make sense of the world around them and learn how to transfer their knowledge to solving new problems. Students begin to see knowledge as malleable. What's more, they see themselves as contributors to the knowledge economy.

Finally, design thinking enables students to see failure as a part of learning and teachers to see setbacks as opportunities for growth. Providing students with needed scaffolds and strategies along the way not only boosts their beliefs about themselves as learners but also enables them to challenge the nature of knowledge and knowing (Dweck, 2017). The tools that students learn and use in the design thinking classroom will benefit them in their other classes and in their life outside school.

The Five Elements of Design Thinking

Each element of the design thinking process is grounded in standards-based learning, rich with embedded formative assessment, and ripe for developing student voice and engagement in the classroom. It's important to remember that the process is fluid and doesn't always follow a linear path. In a sense, design thinking is counter to the mile-wide and inch-deep curriculum in which students accumulate facts and figures while they prepare for summative assessment. Instead, design thinking asks students to consider what questions their understanding can help solve and supports students as they dig deeper to understand the root cause of problems in the world.

Each element has a guiding question. The process of answering is student driven to create intrinsically motivating learning experiences that meet the diverse interests of the learners in our classrooms.

Element 1: Understand and Empathize

In this first element of the design thinking process, students deepen their knowledge through thoughtful assessment, and they exercise empathy and other key social-emotional skills so crucial to student success. By taking perspective and looking more closely at the multiple connections within and among issues, students get acquainted with the complexity of the problems they'll be identifying later on. This introduction to messiness aids in normalizing failure for them, which will be helpful as they begin to test their own proposed solutions to problems.

Understand. Developing understanding is a necessary first step that enables learners to apply their knowledge, but it may also serve as a place where design challenges take hold.

For example, one day after lunch, my students returned to our class to find groups of four desks pushed together, with a tub of water in the center of each group. Also on the grouped tables were rectangular pieces of card stock, parchment paper, pipe cleaners, tape, wooden beads, and tin foil. Not new to my shenanigans, the students looked at me questioningly: What now? I shared the prompt on the chalkboard: "Create an object that will float on water while holding wooden beads."

After a few minutes of playing around with these new tools, my kids got busy building structures sturdy enough to float while holding beads. I watched as they created contraptions and tested them in the basins of water. Fifteen minutes later, four of the groups had come up with a boatlike design; others were either catching on or riffing on successful designs to build their own boats.

I invited students to demonstrate their creations for the class. I also asked them to predict how many wooden beads each boat might hold and to note their findings on the board using tally marks, but without the usual diagonal line that indicates a completed set of five. As I exaggerated the painstaking process of counting each mark one by one, a student questioned why I didn't count by 10. This was a primer into using tally marks and, later, bar graphs; it also foreshadowed a lesson we would visit later in the year when talking about surface area, mass, and weight.

Empathize. Students take on multiple perspectives as they develop empathy or compassion while designing solutions. Teachers can provide tools and processes to aid in this work.

As students work to consider the needs of others, they broaden their worldview, step outside themselves, and learn to observe and listen to others. They learn how to apply their foundational knowledge to helping other people or solving problems in the world.

Element 2: Identify and Research

This phase begins with students isolating the opportunity or concern that their designed solution will address. Students then move into research, where they work to gain a deeper insight into the content.

Identify. Based on understanding content and empathizing with the user, students identify a single problem that their knowledge can help solve. In this way, students dive deeper into content as they grow their sense of competence, efficacy, and autonomy as learners.

Research. Students research the problem in greater detail to determine salient content and identify resources they can turn to for support if they're stuck. This element ensures that students have a sense of agency in their learning while also developing a sense of community as learners collaborate for problem identification.

Element 3: Communicate to Ideate

Students must clearly communicate the ideas they believe have the greatest potential to address the problem and provide valid reasoning as they seek out the most promising idea to prototype. As students grow their voice and sense of competence in learning, teachers support them in providing feedback to their peers and reflecting critically on their own work.

Element 4: Prototype and Test

The fourth element of design thinking includes designing and testing solutions, which requires creativity and successful communication. During this element, students continue to make learning visible by selecting components of their solution and later testing their hypotheses.

Prototype. Students have selected the idea they will bring to the prototype stage and must flesh out all the variables necessary to develop and build it. They must demonstrate deep content knowledge to ensure their prototype meets the needs of the user or system for which it is intended to work.

Test. After building the prototype, students must conduct testing to evaluate how successful their designed solution was in solving their identified problem. Students provide a clear problem statement with specific issues they anticipate their prototype will solve, as well as a list of specific outcomes they will look for in deciding the success of their prototype. Careful observation, clear communication, and receiving and reflecting on feedback are essential components of the element of testing.

Element 5: Iterate and Reflect

By using formative check-ins throughout the design thinking process, teachers foster increasingly complex content knowledge acquisition and ensure that common misconceptions are addressed and are no longer a barrier to acquiring future content knowledge. Students now use feedback based on the testing they did in the fourth element to iterate—that is, revise—their design and reflect on what aspects were most least successful. Iteration and reflection teach the valuable skills of persistence and failing forward while also ensuring students develop strong content knowledge.

Design Thinking in Every Classroom

Regardless of the content or age group, elements of design thinking can be woven throughout instruction in any classroom to deepen learning and engage learners. Consider how design thinking might increase engagement and fuel purposeful learning in your classroom by reflecting on when, where, how, and why you might apply the various elements.

When: Design thinking can live before, during, or after an entire unit of study. Design challenges as a precursor to instruction ensure students are able to apply and understand learning during a unit of instruction. They can also serve as a novel take on an existing unit where students lead the charge in solving problems that affect them most.

Where: Design thinking can live across the curriculum and within every age range. Design thinking encourages kindergartners to tap into their innate curiosity about the world around them while engaging in multimodal learning, just as high school students are called on to use their voice to advocate for meaningful changes in their local and global community. The process of design thinking can apply in living science classrooms where students hone their skills in developing solutions to problems they observe in the world around them or in English language arts classrooms where learners use the power of persuasive writing to raise awareness for a community in need.

How: Using existing curriculum aligned to standards, teachers can ensure that students stay on the pathway to success by providing ongoing formative feedback, a crucial component of design thinking. Chapter 2 details how a simple pivot in your existing curriculum will transform your classroom into an active learning space.

Why: Design thinking is a mechanism for increasing student voice and choice in the classroom. It also encourages empathy, whether toward the individual or system the students are designing solutions for or toward their peers as they provide meaningful feedback. In practicing empathy, we're teaching our students to take perspective, and we're allowing them to take a breath to pause, reflect, and reconsider their role in the learning process.

Built on decades of research in learning science, these elements reinforce what we know to be true: True knowledge acquisition is messy and doesn't live in a silo. The elements of design thinking bring new voices into the design of solutions to our biggest problems and show both our learners and our communities how our combined knowledge is key to a more abundant and just future.

– Notes from the Field –

In 2015, nearly 30 million 15-year-olds across the globe sat for the Programme for International Student Assessment (PISA) administered by the Organisation for Economic Co-operation and Development (OECD). This global assessment is used to measure the math, science, and reading skills of learners worldwide. Students from the consistently high-achieving district of Barrington, Rhode Island, scored at or above global averages, an outcome of great pride but one causing little surprise. It was the recently added student survey around perceptions of learning that was the real eye-opener.

Paula Dillon, the assistant superintendent for learning of the Barrington Schools, was intrigued by one particular question on that survey: "Do you know how you will apply what you are learning now to what you will do in the future?" Dillon noticed that despite their high performance, students were not always certain how their knowledge might aid them in the future. Although the district was doing a good job of preparing students for the assessments, it wasn't doing as well at making that knowledge transferable. As Dillon noted,

"We're looking at the future of work and seeing how automation is replacing traditional jobs, and we knew we had to revise instruction." Seeing this as an opportunity for continued improvement, Dillon set to work engaging her school community in a deep process of self-assessment and revitalization.

Dillon worked with school leaders to develop a theory of action to embrace more experiential learning. The goal was to showcase exceptional teaching and learning throughout the district by highlighting educators engaged in applied learning while also providing embedded coaching in deeper learning and connecting with innovators at institutions such as Northeastern University's Network for Experiential Teaching and Learning (NExT).

The shift to experiential learning required significant changes. Teachers were understandably hesitant. Would they still be able to cover the curriculum if they became more flexible, if they followed the students' lead? During a professional development session at Barrington Middle School, Dillon worked with principal Andrew Anderson to unpack the shift to experiential learning. Together Dillon and Anderson developed a seven-step process that helped guide the work of teacher leaders, administrators, and students embracing this bold shift in practice.

Dillon and Anderson hoped to enact the process first at the middle school and later in the other buildings. Then a small but profound gesture helped assuage any remaining concerns. Thinking on her feet, Dillon quickly scribbled on a piece of paper a message to empower teacher educators. On the paper she simply wrote, "permission slip." This permission slip was addressed to all teachers at Barrington, signed and supported in full by their administrators. It was permission for each educator to freely shift their pedagogy and try something revolutionary—to maintain the same high expectations of student learning across the district by covering the same content through deep experiential learning. In a single moment, Dillon empowered educators to embrace a meaningful change that would transform the district and the lives of every student in it.

In the months that followed, Barrington faculty and staff engaged in hackathons to redesign courses, and Dillon discovered that "the transformation that happened when teachers were allowed to bring creativity was amazing." Parents reported feeling the shift in practice, telling teachers how their kids were coming home eagerly sharing what they were doing each day. When parents asked their children what they had done in school, the word *nothing* vanished from dinner tables across Barrington. Instead, students shared how their learning helped design solutions to local problems. Students built new devices, from robots to a Mars rover; created campaigns to improve social-emotional health; and connected with other learners across the globe.

The experiential learning in Barrington is the cornerstone of design thinking. Each element of the process invites inquiry and problem solving, discovery and evaluation. In the pages that follow, you'll find ideas and protocols to guide your practice through the elements of design thinking, alongside tools to formatively assess and provide feedback to learners. The ingenuity of each element lies in the hand of the ultimate guide on the side—the educator.

As you embark on your journey, I hope you're able to savor each boisterous brainstorming session and relish the anticipatory silence preceding the testing of a newly constructed prototype. May each silent research period in the library result in an even more lively debate during iteration. Moreover, I hope you embrace the intentional messiness of a process where students learn, revise, and grow together. This is the education that John Dewey imagined when he wrote, "Education is not preparation for life; education is life itself."

So here's *your* permission slip: You are hereby permitted to depart from the regularly scheduled program, try something new, and invite your students to play a role in active learning. By doing so, you'll provide meaningful experiences that deepen knowledge acquisition and cultivate curiosity among our youngest citizens.

2
···

Teacher and Student Roles in the Design Thinking Classroom

Today you are You, that is truer than true.
There is no one alive who is Youer than You.

Dr. Seuss

Each fall, the changing leaves are a natural segue into scientific inquiry. As a classroom teacher, I remember collecting a variety of leaves each weekend and returning to my classroom Monday morning to watch eager learners place blank paper atop the leaves and rub with crayons until the entire leaf, veins and all, emerged. We discussed how the shape of the leaf can help identify the type of tree. The leaf's veins were an introduction to deeper concepts about how plants create energy through photosynthesis. Students used many different colors to reproduce on paper the colors that the leaves take on during the fall, including my personal favorite—purple.

It was this divergent color that led to an interesting conversation about which was the leaves' "true" color—the green of the summer or the yellow, orange, or even purple that we see in the fall. One student asked, "But why can't the leaves always be their real colors?" The discussion that followed was about science and individuality. I asked them why leaves were usually green. The students knew at once that photosynthesis was the answer. And I asked them what happens in the fall after the leaves change color. The students knew that the leaves would fall to the ground, and they learned that the tree would hibernate until spring, turning sugar from photosynthesis into starch.

And then one student suddenly remarked, "So the leaves have to cover their real color all summer so they can do their photosynthesis?"

We talked about how the trees were like us, that green is their uniform for working but that they become their true self each fall when they've finished their jobs, just as we might put on comfy clothes when we're home on weekends. Each leaf, like each of us, has a role to play. Together we discussed our roles in school of learning, growing, and supporting one another. Then we talked about how our true colors come out after school and on the weekends, when we're free to play with friends, go to the park, and play games with our family.

Students wondered if we could bring our true colors into the school day, and a beautiful study unfolded. I asked students to write inside the leaves they'd created the things they loved most about their lives—their family, friends, activities, and experiences. These interests ran far deeper than the typical first-day-of-school inventory, and we drew on them throughout the year. On that day my students taught me a powerful lesson: Our classroom roles are more flexible than I'd been taught, and my role as teacher is strengthened when I take the role of the learner. Student leaves also made for a beautiful bulletin board outside our classroom and a reminder that each learner brings different experiences to our shared space every day!

Connecting with Each Student

Just as the true color of leaves doesn't reveal itself until fall, the inner nature of our students' lives is often hidden beneath the surface. Like an iceberg, we see only the very top of who they have become and very little about where they've been, what they believe, and what they hope. Design thinking flips the script from traditional models of education to where student and teacher roles pull from our students' unique interests and experiences in a flexible and fluid manner.

There's an expression that in the classroom "you can't do Bloom before you do Maslow"—that is, before writing curriculum aligned to Bloom's (1956) taxonomy of increasingly complex cognitive functioning, you need to first address students' foundational needs, as presented in Maslow's (1971) hierarchy. Basic needs of food and a place to rest are paramount, but they're followed by other equally important psychological needs—for security, relationships, and self-esteem. A student-led "teacher as guide" approach in the classroom addresses these needs and puts learners on the same team.

Researchers have found much support for what teachers know to be true: that connecting with students reduces disruptions and increases engagement. A recent study showed that small behaviors like greeting students at the classroom door can increase engagement by 20 percent (Cook et al., 2018). The way we build these relationships is a model for how we work with learners as they design solutions for real-world problems.

Career educator and equity, instruction, and literacy coach Zaretta Hammond (2014) provides a primer on how successful learning is predicated on relationships with students in her work *Culturally Responsive Teaching and the Brain*. Quest to Learn teacher Andrea Henkel has seen the power of culturally responsive teaching firsthand, noting, "The most powerful moments I've ever had as a teacher are when the classical hierarchy or power dynamic was removed and replaced with trusting relationships between me and my students." Creating relationships includes inviting students to be co-creators of knowledge. When students identify issues *they* most want to solve, we deepen their motivation while honoring their diverse backgrounds.

In the classroom, it's HEARTS before heads. The students' *home* (H), *educational* experiences (E), *activities* they engage in outside the classroom (A), *reasons* for learning (R), *transformative* life experiences (T), and *special* attributes (S) give a glimpse into the hearts of our learners. As we come to better understand them, we see more clearly how the diverse and dynamic lives they bring to class each day can inform the roles they take throughout each element of design thinking.

Motivation also comes into play here. The acronym CAR—competence, autonomy, and relatedness (Ryan & Deci, 2000)—evokes the fastest, most efficient method for cultivating sustained motivation, and it very aptly applies to teachers and students in a design thinking classroom. Providing students with choice in the way they demonstrate their learning enables them to develop *competence* and flex their sense of *autonomy*. Their learning also promotes *relatedness* because it connects them to the classroom and, ultimately, to the global community. Two recent studies found that inviting students to edit Wikipedia entries shows measurable improvements in their literacy skills and in their ability to understand content-specific terminology (Shane-Simpson, Che, & Brooks, 2016; Walker & Li, 2015). These shifts in teacher and student roles cost nothing more than a leap of faith and a small reorganization of traditional practices.

Mirrors and Windows: Looking into Your Students' Lives

In traditional classrooms, the teacher often dictates learning while students complete their planned work before moving on to new content (see Figure 2.1). These more traditional roles of teacher and student are important, but they often miss two key components: finding meaning in coursework and being able to transfer that learning to other contexts. What's often missing

FIGURE 2.1

Traditional Roles of Teachers and Students

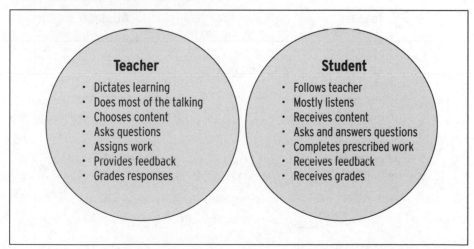

is the iterative and purposeful effort that educators and researchers know enhances, extends, and secures knowledge acquisition (Fandakova & Bunge, 2016; Markant, Ruggeri, Gureckis, & Xu, 2016; Marsh, Arnold, Smith, & Stromeyer, 2015; Moon, 2013).

In design thinking classrooms, the roles of student and teacher fluctuate (see Figure 2.2). They depend on the nature of the learning, student interests, and the structure of the design challenge. The goal is to push our learners and ourselves to do things we feel confident and passionate about but that also seem daunting. Faced with a challenge to resolve, students may design solutions independently, in groups, or in a hybrid form, where they gather to share ideas and then go off to explore novel opportunities to create solutions on their own. In this model, teachers and students *share* in the process of learning.

FIGURE 2.2

Teachers and Students in Design Thinking Classrooms

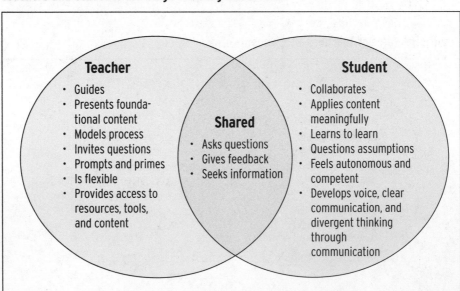

What follows is a series of questions that will better help teachers understand what lies in each of their students' hearts. They serve as both mirrors and windows into the lives of our learners. As students and teachers respond to these questions, they look inward, as though using a mirror, to identify essential aspects of themselves as learners. Likewise, they also learn about all the members of the classroom community, with student responses becoming a window into their various lives. This exercise gives students practice in taking the perspective of others; it also helps identify the unique contributions that members of the class community will make when designing solutions.

HEARTS Before Heads: Questions to Ask Your Students

Home:
- Who are the people in your life who make sure you get to school or to events, help with homework, prepare meals, and talk with you about important things?
- What languages are spoken in your home? By whom?
- What is something unique or interesting about someone with whom you live?

Educational experiences:
- What topics have you *most enjoyed* learning or teaching about in school, and *why*? What made them enjoyable? Was it the subject, the way it was taught, the timing, or the materials? Could you use this learning in other ways?
- What are some topics you have *least enjoyed* learning about in school, and *why*? What made them not enjoyable? Was it the subject, the way it was taught, the timing, or the materials? Or did you not feel prepared to take on this learning?

Activities:
- What after-school activities (clubs, sports, groups) do you participate in, and *why*? What drives you to regularly participate in these activities?

• What do you do when you're not in school and there are no other obligations, and *why*? What makes you enjoy this activity so deeply that you choose to do this in your free time?

Reasons for learning:
• If you had an entire day to do anything or go anywhere, where would you go and what would you do, and *why*? What makes this place, these people, or this space so intriguing to you? Is it the people, the setting, or something it would allow you to do? What would you want to learn from visiting or being in this place?
• What would you like to see your future self doing in 10 years? What type of problems will you be solving, what type of people will you interact with, and in what type of environment would you like to live?

Transformative life experiences:
• What local, national, or global event had an effect on your life? What do you remember about the event? How did it change your thoughts, beliefs, or understandings about the world? How did experiencing this event change you?
• What historical event particularly fascinates you? Does this event elicit curiosity, fear, contempt, or elation? What is most intriguing about this event? What more would you like to understand about it? If you could interview someone who was present at the event, what would you ask them?
• What problem would you like to help solve in your lifetime? What opportunity for change would you like to work on? What do you know about this problem? How did you get interested in this problem? Where would you start in helping to solve it?

Special attributes:
• What is one thing about you that no one in this class knows?
• What is one ability you possess that you are particularly proud of? How did you learn this skill? What has learning this skill taught you?

These question categories are not a recipe but a compass. The goal is to understand each individual's home life, school life, interests, and dreams. Documenting student responses can help you connect content to students' passions and see how their interests and aptitudes can grow throughout the school year. It feels onerous for sure, but once started, it will support you in consistently meeting students where they are and pushing them to where they can be. And when conference season arrives, it's a far richer way of sharing student learning with caregivers than traditional models. You'll be able to provide evidence of the dynamic ways in which learners have collaborated with others, the many tools they've mastered in communicating their knowledge, their areas of content mastery, and the way in which they have engaged purposefully in classroom learning.

Making the Most of Student Responses

Student responses are a valuable source of information that teachers can make full use of throughout the year. The following guidelines will help.

Write questions in language that is contextually, culturally, and developmentally appropriate. Student responses help establish a sense of trust and lay the foundation for strong relationships in the classroom. Questions should be leveled to meet the needs of the diverse learners in the classroom. Younger learners may need to have the text read to them, whereas language learners may need to have the questions translated into their first language. Students with developmental differences may require additional scaffolding.

Encourage students to share their responses and demonstrate mastery in multimodal ways. Students demonstrate mastery in the way they communicate their responses. In early childhood, drawings represent experiences and can be scribed by adults or in collaboration with other emergent writers in the classroom. A makeshift recording studio can be set up with a single computer, tablet, or smartphone so younger learners' voices can shine as they share their stories.

Older, more fluent writers may use traditional paper and pencil or emergent media to respond to prompts. Simple tools like Cardboard Camera, an app that enables users to take virtual reality photos, provide an immersive template for sharing learners' experiences. Tools like Flipgrid enable students to quickly record a video response to prompts, whereas other tools like Seesaw allow for a range of multimedia responses. Podcasts can document both the unique interests and abilities of learners while giving voice to other individuals who are important in their lives. Sketchnotes may help students express more with simple illustrations or clip art than words on a page. By sharing their responses in these ways, students not only demonstrate their varied expertise and interests, but also illuminate ways your time together can best meet their hopes and goals.

Revisit student responses throughout the year. Revisiting student responses to questions throughout the school year allows for new experiences to set the stage for the demonstration of new areas of competence. When I was a teacher, after each assessment I gave students, I would ask them for their feedback on our learning together. Students could either attach a sheet of paper with their responses to the back of the test or reply through a Google Form. Allowing students to anonymously share their experiences about learning—what was most meaningful, what was redundant, what inspired them, what confused or frustrated them—helped me better understand my students' needs and adjust instruction accordingly.

Focus on the *why*. The *why* is the most essential part of each question. It's also the foundation for being both prepared and flexible as teachers and learners. For instance, one little boy in my classroom insisted that of all the subjects he took the previous year, he only liked art class. Had I not explored the comment, I would simply have assigned him the role of illustrator during our design thinking work. However, pulling on that thread further, looking at the *why*, I found out that his interest in art had less to do with art and more to do with the teacher herself. This particular child had a rough time with transitions; the kind way the art teacher used call and response to bring students back from their work was both soothing and effective for him. It was in such stark contrast to his other experiences that art became his favorite subject.

Follow three important rules. Three rules for responding to questions in the HEARTS model can help provide a strong foundation for student and teacher roles in the classroom:

1. Students should share responses to *one question from each category* of the model with their teacher.
2. Students should share *three* responses overall with their peers.
3. Responses should use at least *two different modalities* including, but not limited to, written responses, illustrations, sketchnotes, pictures, videos, audio, and so on.

By making full use of student responses, teachers can better understand and support students in stretching their thinking and celebrating their learning. At the same time, students begin to understand and empathize with one another, creating a truer sense of community in the classroom.

As educators, we must model that learning preferences are pliable over time. Students will come to understand that their roles will change alongside their developing understanding, and, with teacher support, they will demonstrate their developing expertise in ways that make them feel a sense of efficacy in their work.

The Student's HEART and Role

Let's look at the six components of HEARTS—home, educational experience, activities, reasons for learning, transformative life experiences, and special attributes—in terms of the student's role in a design thinking classroom.

Home. A solid understanding of the unique attributes of students' out-of-school lives and how these influence students' access to learning not only sets the foundation for establishing a strong home-to-school connection but also has an impact on student roles in each element of design thinking. Such understanding offers educators more clarity on individual students' access—or lack of access—to other kinds of supports, such as technology or community supports, which will help educators ensure they're working with students to co-design equitable learning experiences.

This understanding also gives educators insights into a more holistic view of a student's identity. For instance, multilingual students and their caregivers can share their language skills in design thinking challenges to bring in a wider audience and highlight the influence of culture on individuals. Honoring the languages used at home enables teachers to celebrate diverse students and also creates a more welcoming environment for caregivers when they visit the classroom. This sets the stage for discussions about culture, language, and identity and helps students connect with one another around both shared and different experiences.

Educational experiences. Understanding the educational experiences each learner brings to the classroom helps teachers meet students where they are and ensure those students are able to reach their highest potential. What's more, a student's educational history invites learners to share the areas they're most proud of and creates opportunities to strengthen areas that need support. Educators discover what students are passionate about, how they like to learn, how they like to get feedback, and the strengths they bring to the group, all of which help them lift student voice as the guiding force for the work, determine the goodness of the fit, and think through group configurations that foster collaboration and communication.

Activities. Just as interests from learning experiences can be drawn on in design thinking classrooms, student engagement in outside activities can drive problem identification and illuminate student connections. Not only can you call out commonalities among students (see this chapter's Notes from the Field), learners can also connect to content in a meaningful way while developing new relationships with peers. Whereas commonalities provide connection points, highlighting uniqueness among students celebrates the diversity they represent as a group and is helpful in developing students' empathy and strengthening their capacity for perspective taking.

Reasons for learning. Student responses to the questions in this section reveal what matters most to them. This information helps teachers weave into the work the most important parts of each learner's hopes, dreams, and goals throughout the school year. These responses also shed light on the problems that are most important in students' lives. Such insights help educators find connections between student passions and content, deepen relationships within the classroom, and help students find purpose in their work.

Transformative life experiences. Many creative takes on this question have been used as an icebreaker at the start of each new school year. For example, in the game Two Truths and a Lie, students must each share two facts and one lie about themselves—and their peers or teacher must decide which is the lie. Students may share a surprising experience that shaped their current beliefs, provide a spark of inspiration to others, or even serve as a connector between two students with seemingly distinct interests, backgrounds, or understandings within the same classroom community.

Special attributes. Many students may wish to respond publicly to the questions in this section because it's an opportunity to share information that allows them to feel unique and celebrated. Because the nature of the questions here is a bit more personal—for example, "What is one thing about you that no one in this classroom knows?"—some students might wish to share their responses directly with you. They may be seeking support or connection with you and may share very different responses than those that are made publicly. Student responses, whether public or private, are a powerful way to fully celebrate and support each learner.

The Teacher's HEART and Role

Now let's look at the six components of HEARTS in terms of the teacher's role in a design thinking classroom.

Home. As educators, we're often seen as mythical creatures by our students, and mostly, we hope, in a positive light! Sharing information about your home life—from your daily responsibilities to your cultural background and upbringing—in a professional but meaningful way invites students to take perspective from your vantage point, just as you have taken perspective from theirs. It also enables students to find areas of commonality and develop trust with you as their teacher.

I once heard a story about a teacher who was reticent to share personal information with her school community. Not wanting to bring her own experiences into the classroom, this teacher didn't divulge that her daughter was fighting a rare bone cancer. Although this educator threw herself into meeting her students' needs during class time, she was also working hard outside the classroom to support her struggling family. It was only when she took extended leave to help her daughter get through treatment that her school community finally learned of this struggle. When the teacher returned to school after her daughter's treatment, each member of the community greeted her wearing superhero outfits, representing both the generous non-family member who saved her daughter's life as a marrow donor and (I'd like to think) the incredibly brave and powerful teacher who steadily supported both her home and school families. All of this is to say that sharing information about the individuals in your home, from your pet rabbit to your roommates, shows our humanness and opens the door to the empathy we want our students to demonstrate in our classrooms each day.

Opening up this way allowed me many opportunities to connect with my own students. During a book club I used to run during lunch, a student from Turkey was thrilled to see me eating pita bread with za'atar, a Middle Eastern spice, and it launched us into a conversation about the spices her grandmother used in making grape leaves. At parent-teacher night, one parent commented how funny it was to hear her child using a Yiddish term when the child was flummoxed (*verklempt*) with the homework. Similarly, when I had to miss school in observance of a holiday, it was an opportunity to share my culture with my students. We made the connection among the various harvest celebrations in different cultures, shedding light on the ways that we're different and the ways that we're the same.

Educational experiences. Sharing your own learning experiences is prime time for showing that you, too, are always learning. What's more, you can model your problem-solving practices and share information about the additional supports that help you grow as a learner. These conversations invite students to ask questions about *your* skills, an opportunity they don't frequently have.

When working with young students, I like to share my experiences as a child learning to read through songs. Teaching graduate students, I shared the truth about learning in a Big 10 school where the cavernous lecture halls made me feel lost and confused. Oftentimes, I would share stories about my successes or challenges teaching the same course in previous years and reflect on the ways it felt least and most successful. In being vulnerable, I was able to connect with my students and model that we're all a work in progress as we strive for the best environmental fit for our work.

Activities. Just as student interests serve as launching points for inquiry and discovery, so, too, will your areas of expertise bring more students into learning as they see how some of your experiences may match their own. Sharing your own passion for school-based activities, from coaching the soccer team to running a crew for the school play, establishes relatedness throughout the class community and increases the type of content you can call on when providing examples for design projects.

Reasons for learning. Teacher responses to this question can demonstrate that learning is never-ending and that our goals grow with each new year. Your responses can also reinforce student resilience in the face of setbacks, as students see firsthand how you solve problems or carve out time for yourself and those you love. Oftentimes this invites students to share ways in which they have expertise that supports these goals and builds classroom community.

Nowhere was this more evident than in my role as a professor in a teacher education program. My adult students taught me how I could visit far-off lands through technology and how, using a website that tracks airfares, I could see when that dream trip to the Galápagos Islands might be within reach. By sharing what you would want to learn or explore if you were given the gift of a day without restraints, you're modeling opportunities for designed solutions, from creating a virtual tour of the Galápagos Islands in science class to learning how to use new editing tools to become a more skilled artist.

Transformative life experiences. Each of us brings unique interests, abilities, talents, and dreams to the classroom. Remembering your individuality both inspires your students and helps you create more meaningful learning. A transformational moment I once shared with students was a conversation with my grandmother, a Holocaust survivor. I recalled how in my childhood I learned about the number tattoo on my grandmother's arm, which led me down a path toward advocacy and social justice. Learning about my family's history changed my students' perspectives about me; they saw me both as a child like them and as a person whose connection to the past has changed her future.

Special attributes. Unique attributes are already in your classroom, from the mug you use for coffee to the pen you carry to share feedback on student work. You could share a moment of pride or a way in which you're more similar to your students than they think. Sharing your unique attributes creates a dynamic classroom community where each individual is respected and valued as an individual.

Tying It All Together

Understanding student interests, motivations, and areas needing strengthening helps create roles in the design thinking classroom and in the systems for feedback that will support students as they deepen understanding (Rands & Gansemer-Topf, 2017; Ruzek et al., 2016). For instance, knowing that certain students prefer more active ways of learning, whereas others prefer quieter and more reflective experiences apart from the group, enables you to establish environments that support student preferences and increase motivation (National Research Council, 2003). Responses also provide an opportunity to broaden each student's cognitive toolbox by presenting novel opportunities outside their comfort zone, from working with peers to solve problems to using new technologies.

The questions we pose for students provide an insight into what motivates, inspires, or frustrates them and serve as a framework for clarifying expectations during elements of design thinking. The framework outlined in Figure 2.3 is a culmination of student responses and can be applied to specific elements of the design thinking process—each of which we'll unpack throughout the coming chapters—or to the design thinking classroom more generally.

FIGURE 2.3

Framework for Student and Teacher Expectations

Teacher Role	Student Role
Q: What problems will your design address?	
Scaffold problem identification based on student interest, curiosity, and areas of concern.	Select problem developed from an understanding of yourself, your peers, and the world around you.
Q: What will you *do* during each element?	
Encourage students to try other ways of solving problems, use new tools, and think through the perspective of another. Encourage flexible grouping, and support exploration of topics students may not have otherwise considered.	Identify areas of strength and those needing support. Meaningfully apply content to areas born out of curiosity and wondering.
Q: How will you *collaborate* with others?	
Who can learn from and with whom? Who has experiences that will enrich the experiences of others?	What areas of strength do you bring, what do your peers bring, how will you ensure every voice is heard, and how will you resolve conflict?
Q: *How* will you submit work?	
Provide different ways of documenting work. Allow space for ongoing projects to live.	Understand the process for submitting work. Take ownership in submitting and sharing work with your peers and teacher.
Q: How will you *seek* feedback?	
Regularly check in with students. Use exit tickets: How did that feel? What areas are confusing? How do you need support? Provide ways for students to ask questions outside the classroom (e-mail address) and anonymously (question box), and set aside time during class for questions.	Identify how, when, and where you are receiving and providing feedback.
Q: How will you *give* feedback?	
Model the modalities of learning in providing feedback by showing both written responses and visual responses.	Use the modalities you know—and always try to grow.

(continued)

FIGURE 2.3

Framework for Student and Teacher Expectations *(continued)*

Teacher Role	Student Role
Q: *When* will you receive feedback?	
Establish timing for when you will provide learner feedback. Determine how students can ask for feedback if they need it sooner. Clarify when feedback may take longer to provide.	Stay accountable to yourself and peers by sticking to the time frame for providing feedback to your peers and teacher about your ongoing work.
Q: What are you expected *to do* with feedback?	
What are your expectations about responding to feedback? What is the process for students to revise their work or thoughts before, during, and after a design challenge?	Know the teacher's expectations about responding to feedback. Understand the process and take ownership of responding if resubmissions are allowed.
Q: What do you do *when you're stuck*?	
How will you call the class back if they seem off track? What general scaffolds can you provide for students who need additional support? What tools can you share or skills can you preteach as areas of support?	How might you solve problems before seeking out a peer or teacher? What "more knowledgeable others" are in your class or community? How will you seek out the teacher for feedback? What ways are you most comfortable reaching out to peers or teachers for support?

– Notes from the Field –

MaryRose Joseph is a high school science teacher and certified building administrator in Chappaqua, New York. Every school year when her students arrive to class, she tries out new ways to build community while honoring the unique attributes of the learners in her classroom. One fall morning, she started an activity where students were asked to identify something unique to them as individual learners. Students quickly listed areas of pride that set them apart first as individuals, then as pairs, as a classroom, and later as an entire school community. This process demonstrated the way learners are connected to others within the classroom and the greater school community, allowing students to take the perspective of others and, in doing so, establishing a strong foundation of empathy and understanding of their peers. This is a skill that is continuously honed in the elements of design thinking as learners collaboratively solve problems and grow together by honoring the voices and experiences of other. After more than two decades as an educator and instructional leader, Joseph understands that empowering students to learn about one another is the key to creating a safe and inclusive classroom where learning flourishes.

Jay Billy is an elementary school principal and a catalyst for empowered and innovative educators in New Jersey. His creativity is limitless and is matched only by his desire to support educators with best practices in building school community. One of my favorite exercises he does is part of the school's getting-to-know-you routine in the fall. Billy asks students to take a scrap piece of paper and write one thing about them that nobody in the class knows. Then he asks them to crumple that paper up into a ball. Once all the students hold crumpled papers in their hands, he shouts, "Snowball fight!" Billy leads by example, tossing his paper playfully across the room, quickly picking up another paper to continue the snowball fight. After a few minutes, he asks students to pick up the snowball closest to them and, one after the other, to read the statement aloud and guess who it describes.

This activity helps learners identify who is great at certain crafts, sports, languages, or musical instruments. It also translates into a network of experts that students can access during design thinking challenges. What Billy and many other inspirational educators know is that building relationships through playful learning results in deeper learning. By empowering his students and staff to be playful, he invites them to take risks that lead to powerful growth.

Amber Coleman-Mortley was a college athlete before teaching physical education and health and later advocating for educators, parents, and civics education. Her years of experience have given her an extensive inventory of ways to invite learners to share their passions and honor the many voices in the classroom. Her depth of knowledge in education is why she was so inspired by the way her daughter's classroom teacher sought to celebrate the uniqueness of each learner in an activity called Me Soup. The teacher asked the children to bring in three items that represented them, things they would use to create a *me soup*. Coleman-Mortley's daughter brought in a lacrosse stick, a drumstick, and a video game console. Sitting together in class, each child shared their "ingredients" and learned about their shared connections and about the exciting ways they differed. "My daughter was no longer just another girl but was the gamer and the lacrosse player, and the kids started asking her questions," recalls Coleman-Mortley. These small but compelling pieces of information about each student empowered learners with the competence, autonomy, and relatedness they needed to feel connected and integral to the class community.

How Not to Recreate the Wheel:
Same Objectives, Different Pathways

You haven't seen a tree until you've seen its shadow from the sky.

Amelia Earhart

Rebecca Henderson runs the robotics/STEAM studio at Barrington Middle School in Rhode Island. Her students learn to use a variety of tools, from 3D printers to 3Doodler pens to robotic tools such as Cubelets and Spheros. One day she introduced students to a new tool, a set of NXT robots. As students began discussing the language they might use to program their new tool, a student suddenly shouted, "It looks like WALL-E!"

Then the discussion took off. Students recalled the animated film where the waste-collecting robot falls in love with a search robot named EVE; the students were frustrated that the two robots were not able to get married in the film. Henderson took a deep breath and asked, "Do you want to have a wedding for them in class?" Students didn't skip a beat before answering *yes!*

Students needed to learn to code this new tool to prepare for the wedding that would happen in only a few weeks' time. They worked diligently and had to get answers to many questions before they could tackle the project. How would the robots park in the pews? Who would write the vows? How would the robots move from the ceremony to the reception? How would the robots move to the (allergy-free) tables to gather their dinners? Who would choose the music, and how would robots move in sync for the first dance? As Henderson noted, "If I had come into class and told my students to plan a wedding for their robots, they would have laughed. But suddenly, my kids are arguing about whether the robots needed to have a religion to say their vows!"

The process wasn't without its struggles. At one point, several groups were ready to quit working as teams, but then they charted out the jobs that needed to be done, regrouped, and worked on their allotted tasks to learn to code, iterate, and ultimately put on a robot wedding in their classroom. The event created such a buzz that parents and community members wanted to join. The students set up a photo booth where participants, including building administrators, were photographed with the robots to celebrate the event.

What began as a simple lesson in coding turned into a schoolwide experience. Students were able to apply their learning in this intriguing way because Henderson had created a safe environment where they could ask questions and be curious. Because the students were allowed to guide inquiry in the classroom, they learned far more than what the few standards aligned to the coding demanded. They mastered complex code, gained essential communication skills, and exercised the critical thinking and creativity required to solve important problems.

Learning Through Applying

Distinct from pure discovery learning, design thinking is a guided approach to understanding *the application of content as it is learned*. To be clear, this perspective of design thinking doesn't ask students to discover the content but, instead, presents content in a clear and guided way and asks students to find meaning through applying their knowledge to design solutions.

Most educators are already using aspects of design thinking in their classrooms when asking students to apply, synthesize, and create on the basis of their learning. Therefore, translating standards-based curriculum to invite in elements of design thinking does not require additional teaching. Instead, reframing the curriculum means teaching concepts iteratively using ongoing formative assessment, with a focus on the utility of the content. Although there's no single recipe for translating curriculum into design thinking experiences, there *is* a single overarching question to ask yourself and your students: You've learned it; now what are you going to do with it?

Reframing the curriculum is not synonymous with reinventing the curriculum. It just requires looking at what currently exists through a new lens, beginning with the standards. Curricular standards are the goalposts, large and wide guides for planning meaningful learning experiences. Not only do standards vary wildly by state and grade level, but they also don't dictate the pathways toward learning.

The curriculum is the pathway that provides students with the transdisciplinary knowledge essential for critical thinking, collaboration, communication, and conflict resolution. Design thinking is a way of enacting curricular standards through experiences that place the *why* of learning in the shared hands of both learners and educators. This means that a unit that typically includes six days of direct instruction may have just one day of direct instruction in the design thinking model, with five days of scaffolded research, ideation, testing, and reflection.

Just as there's no one-size-fits-all approach to enacting standards through curriculum and instruction, there's no drag-and-drop method for developing design thinking classrooms. It's also not an all-or-nothing approach. You can begin experimenting with these methods by rethinking one unit of curriculum or a single lesson plan, or following the interests of the diverse learners in your classroom to identify an opportunity for reframing the nature of teaching and learning.

Reframing the Curriculum: Questions to Consider

In this chapter, we're going to focus on the questions we need to consider as educators in reframing our curriculum for design thinking. Before inviting students to use their learning to design solutions to the problems around them, consider the following questions, which are drawn from research on successful pedagogy (Darling-Hammond, 2008):

- **Clear goals and expectations:** Do students know the goal of their learning, and are they clear about the expectations of their work? Where will students seek out additional information if they get stuck? How will students receive feedback from me and from their peers?

- **Contextually relevant content:** Can this content be connected to the unique experiences of learners in my classroom? How can I use what I know about my learners to more deeply connect them to this learning and draw them into more meaningful design experiences?
- **Experiences aligned to curriculum:** How are my students meeting the curricular goals and learning standards while enacting design thinking? In what ways are their experiences extending the standards and goals from previous years?
- **Opportunities to practice:** How will I support my students by providing multiple ways to demonstrate mastery? What fail-safes will I put into place for when my students struggle or when they're ready for deeper learning?
- **Ongoing support for learning (formative assessment):** Are there multiple opportunities throughout the process to provide feedback to students? What are my expectations for how students use feedback? How will I support students who wish to change their work as a result of this feedback? What tools will I provide for students to share their successes and struggles with me and others? What tools will I invite students to share that give them voice and agency in their work?

Adding the design thinking lens to the development of curriculum is distinct from many methods of instruction. For instance, in more traditional modes of instruction, rote questions and responses are differentiated at best but rigidly uniform at worst. Design thinking takes a different approach; it asks students to identify problems they find worthy to solve in the world around them. What's more, design thinking goes beyond the problem to invite learners to take the perspective of others in designing solutions because it uses constructivist theory, where learner and teacher are co-constructors of knowledge. Constructivist classrooms bring forth the experiences of teachers and learners as a way to enhance and extend inquiry (Oliver, 2000). Teachers and students may share the role of guide; student roles may also include that of pioneer in actively creating new knowledge.

Rethinking the current curriculum means changing not the standards but rather the *delivery* of the aligned content. For instance, although knowledge acquisition in a design thinking curriculum requires preteaching and reteaching of concepts, concepts are differentiated and student agency guides learning. And when students are asked to find ways to apply their knowledge in meaningful ways to design solutions, their cognitive toolbox grows.

Start Small to Go Big

The vignette about the robots at the beginning of this chapter is a prime example of an area ripe for a first foray into design thinking. The road toward the robot wedding was not a linear progression toward learning objectives but, instead, a messy and often deeper dive into the content. Students had to learn coding skills beyond the scope of the anticipated learning goals, and this learning was driven entirely by student interest. What's more, the students struggled to determine the roles of their peers in enacting this celebration. Who would be responsible for the seating arrangement, planning the music, and transporting the robots? Each assignment required complex coding, from getting the robots to dance to the predetermined songs, to getting them to move from one location to the next.

As they deepened their coding skills, students also learned how to resolve conflict with teacher support and collaborate with peers, improving their communication skills along the way. Henderson invited student-driven inquiry around existing learning goals; what followed was a unit far more complex than she imagined on advanced coding, relationship building, and teamwork.

Where to Begin

To set the stage for a successful foray into design thinking, consider your existing curriculum and select a small but meaningful place to start. Think back to your previous teaching experiences and ask yourself, when were students *curious* about the content? When were they *confused?* When were they *connected?* Areas of instruction where students are curious, confused, or connected are ripe for beginning design thinking work.

Curiosity

Building off students' curiosity often provides built-in motivation for sustained engagement. Much research supports the use of curiosity in the classroom as an impetus for deeper engagement, from providing surprising information to adolescents (Clark & Seider, 2017) to inviting questions from students to extend inquiry in early childhood classrooms (Chouinard, 2007; Engel, 2011). Work by acclaimed pedagogue Paulo Freire (2018) suggests educators foster what he calls "critical curiosity" through solving realistic problems, which also provides a deeper understanding of social justice issues, an essential element of student learning. In fostering students' critical curiosity, learners unpack issues of justice and equity in their own lives and communities while learning about the world outside their town.

Confusion

Building from areas of students' innate curiosity may feel too easy, like low-hanging fruit. Perhaps you want a more challenging starting point, in which case, beginning with an area of confusion may be an ideal place to dive into the messy and exciting experience of shifting curriculum, where learners take on the role of problem solver as they work toward designing solutions. One group of middle school students struggled to distinguish between the different forms of democracies (e.g., direct, representative, participatory, pluralist). Connecting each form of democracy to their student government allowed students to identify the benefits and downfalls of each model and, in doing so, invited a change in the structure of their student council from participatory to direct democracy. Building from confusion, students rebuilt their representation to invite more student voice and choice into their time at school. Launching into design thinking based on an area of confusion is not only great practice but also supported by a raft of research in cognitive science in which disequilibrium is seen as a precursor to deeper learning (Craig,

Graesser, Sullins, & Gholson, 2004; D'Mello, Lehman, Pekrun, & Graesser, 2014).

Connection

Setting the stage for the types of collaboration and creative thinking required by design thinking is infinitely more powerful when students have a personal connection with the content. Research shows that when students make connections to content on the basis of lived experiences or prior knowledge, it enhances both learning and engagement while building stronger recall (Hulleman & Harackiewicz, 2009; Rohrer & Taylor, 2006).

How to Translate Existing Units into Design Thinking Projects

Your curriculum is begging to be transformed by design thinking. Don't believe me? Take a moment to look at the scope and sequence for your domain or grade level, sift through the overarching units, or flip back to the previous month of instruction in your plan book. Can you recall a time when students were more curious, confused, or connected to content than usual?

Most likely, you can. You probably naturally enacted elements of design thinking, not to reconstruct the curriculum, but rather to reframe it to support your students.

Based on your observations, select a single lesson to test the design thinking waters. Or, if you wish to work with an entire unit, dive into the following exercise. The questions listed below will help pull out the essential features from your finely honed instruction as you reframe your curriculum:

- **Subject:** Unit/lesson of instruction
  — What standard(s) does the unit/lesson address?

- **Learning:** Objectives, progressions, domains of development
  — What are the specific learning objectives?
  — How do students demonstrate mastery of each learning objective?
  — What do typical learning progressions look like as students approach mastery of each learning objective? In what ways are students

physically, social-emotionally, and cognitively engaged during this unit of instruction? How can you include students in identifying the problems that this learning will solve that will also feed into their designed solutions?

- **Assessments:** Demonstrating mastery
  — Where do your check-ins or formative assessments live within this instruction? What are students asked to do at each checkpoint? How will this learning tie into their designed solutions?
  — What are the formal assessments? What are students asked to do to demonstrate mastery? How are students asked to reflect on the process of designing solutions and on each element of their experience to reinforce both soft and hard skills and secure lasting understanding?

- **Timing and content connections**
  — What is the time frame for instruction?
  — How does this instruction relate to prior knowledge?
  — How does this instruction connect to future learning?

Content, standards, and timing remain constant in reframing the curriculum for design thinking. What shifts is the *pace of learning* and *the way students demonstrate mastery* toward your learning goals. Often the pace at which students learn concepts increases as students move toward their goals. In Henderson's class, learners quickly moved past existing standards as they worked to code the complex patterns of movement the robots would follow.

Along with a student-centered shift in pacing comes a deeper demonstration of mastery. This mastery demonstration is supported by providing ongoing formative feedback to learners in a way that fosters continuous growth. Once you've identified the standards and objectives, you can delineate how student learning progresses toward mastery.

Domains of Development, Objectives, and Progressions

The way teachers reframe learning standards into experiential learning is the true magic in rethinking curriculum through the lens of design thinking.

It begins by acknowledging the essential components for learning and supporting students in finding ways where their knowledge can make them designers of solutions. There's no formula for transforming objectives into designed solutions because what inspired one group of students this year may fall flat another year. What *is* essential is supporting students as they identify how their learning applies to solving real-world problems.

Let's look at domains of development, learning objectives, and progressions in the context of reframing your curriculum.

Domains of development. Although the myth of learning styles has been widely dispelled (Kirschner, 2017; Riener & Willingham, 2010), the varying perspectives and interests students bring to the classroom should nevertheless be a foundation for applying multimodal learning. Learning is a result of three overarching domains: physical, social-emotional, and cognitive. Design thinking integrates these domains.

The *physical domain* includes the specific actions the learner takes to acquire knowledge, from quietly listening to a sonnet, to manipulating puzzle pieces, to singing an arpeggio. Students' beliefs about learning (epistemology); feelings about their ability to learn (efficacy); reasons why they believe they're successful (attributions); motivations to learn (orientation); and ability to take perspective and potentially empathize are some of the many aspects of the *social-emotional domain* (Bernacki, Nokes-Malach, & Aleven, 2015; Butler & Shibaz, 2014; Hofer, 2016; Lin-Siegler, Dweck, & Cohen, 2016). The *cognitive domain* includes both domain-specific skills (e.g., math, history, art) and domain-general skills (e.g., calculating, positioning, drawing) that demonstrate the ability to connect content learned in a science class to learning in an art class (e.g., "Why yes! That Klari Reis painting on a petri dish is a representation of spilled milk").

When reframing curriculum, it's important to consider ways to engage all three of these overarching (and overlapping) domains of development, as students can demonstrate each one of them in the process of designing solutions. Here are some examples of actions they might take in each of the three domains:

- Physical: Constructing, manipulating, creating, planning, drawing
- Social-emotional: Discussing, explaining, finding consensus, collaborating
- Cognitive: Explaining, creating, describing, comparing and contrasting, developing an argument

Learning objectives. Not every learning objective is an ideal fit for design thinking solutions. Collaborating with students to identify the *purpose* and *utility* of classroom learning to real-world applications is the first step in rethinking curriculum to invite designed solutions.

Consider the following questions as you think about how you might shift learning objectives to activate design thinking in your classroom:

- What is the most important aspect of the objective?
  — Is it *really* important that a student draw a certain amount of arrays or write a certain number of words?
  — How can my students and I brainstorm the many problems this knowledge may solve, and how might I enable learners to use these needs as the impetus for the designed solutions?

- What is most essential for students to be able to *do* after learning this specific objective?
  — What behaviors are the most salient evidence of learning?
  — How will these behaviors connect learners' designed solutions to the learning objectives?

- What is my role in helping students master this objective?
  — How much of my instruction should be direct instruction, group work, and independent work?
  — Where can I scaffold support, and how can I engage learners in taking the role of expert?

- How will my learning objectives help students create solutions across content and grade levels?
  — Art: Will students be able to take the perspective of those who came before?

— English: Will students be able to communicate more effectively with others through writing from different perspectives?

— Math: Will students be able to manipulate data to predict the impact of a storm using models?

— Music: Will students be able to infer the affect of the composer or the culture from the choice of musical key?

— Science: Will students be able to extend their knowledge of taxonomy in life sciences to organizing knowledge in earth sciences?

— Social studies: Will students be able to distinguish the influence of primary and secondary sources on citizen voting patterns?

• What resources will students access to gain deeper insight into these problems?

— Should I share specific resources with students all at once, or should students receive content over time throughout the designed solution?

— Should students be responsible for identifying requisite content to solve the problem, and how will they be supported in seeking this information?

— Should resources be shared through direct instruction, small-group instruction, or on an as-needed basis?

• How will the process of designing solutions affect students' perspectives, improve their engagement with others and with the content, and extend inquiry?

In the earlier grades, it's helpful to provide a starting point for designed solutions, but as students move into secondary education, they will identify the problem they wish to take on, increasing ownership. For instance, a standard high school–level world language class states that *students will develop cross-cultural skills and understandings*. This standard can be translated into the following learning objective: *Students will simulate an encounter between two friends in a target language culture, using appropriate social conventions, gestures, and body language.*

Although the hope is that students can communicate in a culturally appropriate way in a target language, the *why* is still missing. To translate this objective into a design thinking experience, the new objective may ask students to *use the target language to describe life in our community to someone visiting our community for the first time*. In the redesigned objective, as students actively use the target language, they experience firsthand how gestures and social conventions of the target language connect to their own language while taking the perspective of another student. This solution moves beyond a simple role-play; it requires a deeper understanding of social conventions, gestures, and body language that may be unique to different cultures.

Learning progressions. Learning progressions are the small steps learners make as they move toward mastering each learning objective. They're the baby steps that go into understanding the gestures unique to the target language in the high school objective above. Similar to the zone of proximal development (Vygotsky, 1978), learning progressions enable students to learn different concepts in developmentally appropriate times and with careful scaffolding by more knowledgeable others.

Research on learning progressions is often an attempt to clarify misconceptions inherent in specific content areas and to suggest specific benchmarks on the road toward demonstrating content mastery. Some researchers consider learning progressions to be more like progress maps during learning (Masters & Forster, 1996), whereas others suggest a requisite set of building blocks for content mastery (Popham, 2007). Learning progressions are often predicated on a systematic way of learning content as students develop mastery, and some research indicates normative progressions that vary by domain (Smith, Wiser, Anderson, & Krajcik, 2006).

Figure 3.1 offers an example of how you might translate your learning objectives into learning progressions. Notice that the steps are unique to a specific design thinking experience—that of the robot wedding. This simple visual enables you to map formative and summative feedback so you can seamlessly apply it throughout the design thinking process.

Take a moment to consider the many small steps your students take in understanding the content you've chosen for your foray into design thinking.

Each step in their learning progression provides opportunities for rich formative assessment throughout design thinking experiences, ensuring just-in-time feedback to support student learning.

FIGURE 3.1

Translating a Learning Objective into a Learning Progression

Students move from left to right as they work to master the learning objective: Students will use coding skills to create a robot wedding where 2 robots and 10 guests move from ceremony to reception.

Map the experience. Identify code to move robots sequentially. Select roles for different students and robots (e.g., participants, officiant, betrothed). Map roles onto specific tasks (e.g., seating, music, placement of robots).	Use the map to chart distance from one place to the next (e.g., ceremony to reception). Select codes that will allow robots to move to their positions. Check in with students/robots to see if they're on track to fulfill their roles (e.g., different positions during wedding, music selection).	Code robots and practice moving them from one place to the next. Learn complex codes to enact different movements from procession to dance moves. Regulate one another's work to ensure everyone is prepared for the big day. Hold dress rehearsals to practice the robots' moves for the big day.	Robot wedding is attended by fellow students, parents, administrators, and faculty. Student robots enact complex codes to successfully move from one place to the next through the ceremony and reception.
Standards: Science/CSTA/ELA/21st century skills	**Standards:** Science/CSTA/ELA/21st century skills	**Standards:** Science/CSTA/ELA/21st century skills	**Standards:** Science/CSTA/ELA/21st century skills

Objectives that have been reframed to invite flexible pathways and dynamic solutions meet standards while also engaging students in meaningful work. Using learning progressions to clarify the knowledge students demonstrate on their pathway toward mastering objectives requires considering the following aspects of the content:

- What are essential understandings of the content?
- What are the different skills that are fundamental for understanding?
- What previous content is embedded within this learning?
- What concepts are particularly simple for learners to grasp within this content?
- Where do your students typically struggle in learning this content?
- What are the common misconceptions within this content?
- What supports have been helpful in elucidating these misconceptions (e.g., animations, visual aids, illustrations, experiments)?

Your responses to these questions provide the framework for rethinking your instruction and serve as a compass for formative and summative assessment. Think about how you can use your existing scaffolds and check-ins to meet students where they typically struggle or how you can give students more autonomy in areas that require less scaffolding. Based on areas of struggle, you might repurpose direct instruction into small-group work and differentiated instruction with student prompts. Similarly, you might provide brief minilessons before releasing students to research and continue in their designing.

Looking at curriculum through the lens of design thinking requires identifying concepts that are essential to teach in a traditional manner and allowing students to practice their understanding through their designed solution. For instance, instead of providing direct instruction for coding each dance, Henderson provided foundational understanding of how to code specific actions. Students were then able to use that knowledge to create more complex movements.

By now, you've probably identified a single area where you might begin the design thinking process. After giving it some thought, you may have identified the learning objectives, the learning progressions, and the developmental domains addressed. It's time to align the learning progressions toward mastery to create the formative and summative assessments you'll use in design thinking.

Feedback for the Win

A key issue with design thinking is not the engagement or eagerness of students to create solutions but rather the ability of the educator to capture evidence of the deep learning that goes into the process. Traditional forms of assessment are often inadequate in capturing the different ways students acquire and apply knowledge in real time, and even more innovative forms of assessment are often not implemented in a way that reflects deep learning. For these reasons, it's paramount to define indicators of success before engaging in the design thinking process.

Goldilocks: Not Too Little, Not Too Much

Just as the design thinking process requires beginning with perspective taking, so, too, does the development of assessments used during design thinking. Too many pauses for assessment break the flow of great work; too few, and there's little evidence that this shift is positively affecting student learning and engagement.

To prepare to document learning and celebrate growth, consider the following:

- How will students demonstrate their learning?
  - Although students may previously have solved math problems or written a persuasive essay, in the design thinking experience, will they be creating structures, filming a public service announcement to change hearts and minds, or printing a 3D model as a prototype?

- How will you formatively assess student work?
  - Are you circulating the room to have informal conversations with students to check for understanding?
  - Do you collect exit tickets; ask students to submit a video response to a prompt; or ask for a quick show of thumbs up, thumbs down, or thumbs sideways?

- How do you summatively assess student work?
  - Do students take a final test or submit a portfolio, essay, or some other form of work product?

— Do students submit work online or in class?

• What constitutes mastery?
— Does the work receive a certain score? If so, what score constitutes passing?

• Are students invited to resubmit their work?
— What is your process for allowing students to do so?

Reframing assessment begins with rethinking the way students demonstrate mastery. Where are the formative and summative assessments in your instruction? What is it about these assessments that informs your students' learning and your instruction? This requires breaking down each formative and summative assessment to identify which components are essential in demonstrating mastery. Using the learning progressions identified previously, you can map the formative and summative assessments in supporting learners as they move toward mastery.

Supporting Students Through Formative Assessments

Checking in with students supports ongoing learning and helps take the temperature of learners in the classroom. You're not simply assessing the content—you're assessing the way students are collaborating, communicating, or feeling about the progress of their work. Most formative assessment methods are not content or age specific; they can provide you with a quick read of the room and set learners up for success.

Formative assessments can be given the moment students are seated or as they leave for the day. The distinguishing feature of these assessments is that you're using student responses to modify your instruction and support. For instance, a quick formative check-in with "fist to five" enables students to quickly assess and share their degree of confidence about a given topic area, from "no confidence" (fist) to "ready to go" (all five fingers). This is a visual indicator of how prepared students are to embark on their purposeful mission. It also prepares you to meet students at their times of confusion as they move through the learning progression. Other assessments, such as "3-2-1"— in which students might share three things they learned during class time, two things they find confusing or surprising, and one thing they wish they could revisit the following day—are terrific at the end of class to help you prepare for the following day.

Raising Student Voice with Summative Assessments

Although ongoing feedback helps support learners, summative assessment ensures that students have acquired meaningful content throughout the learning experience. It's important to note that designed solutions are often not a summative assessment. In the instance of the robot wedding, the main event was a synthesis of multiple formative assessments throughout the experience, but that event didn't require students to synthesize their learning to demonstrate mastery. Figure 3.2 shows how you might add formative and summative assessments to support students throughout their learning progressions.

Summative assessments are not synonymous with a multiple-choice test; they can be flexible to invite student choice. Nicki Didicher (2016) invites learners to select from a "bento and buffet" model, where students demonstrate content mastery at the end of instruction by selecting assessment methods from multiple multimodal categories. Flexible summative assessments can range from choice boards to "menus" from which students choose a preferred assessment among appetizers, main courses, and desserts. Students can select one assessment per column on a board or complete a row of responses (think Tic-Tac-Toe or Bingo). Such assessments highlight the many modalities of learning while celebrating the unique ways in which students enjoy demonstrating their knowledge (see Figure 3.3).

To create more flexible summative assessments, consider embedding the following questions as part of your assessments.

Content connections:
- How was this content related to something you had learned before in our class?
- How was this content related to something you had learned in another class or in another grade?

FIGURE 3.2

Adding Assessments to Learning Progressions

Learning objective: Students will create a robot wedding for 2 robots and 10 guests.

Small Steps
Students create seating charts, map the distance from ceremony to reception, select music, identify robot roles (e.g., participants, officiant, betrothed).

Formative Assessment
Four corners: Move to a (labeled) corner of the room that aligns with your interest.
3-2-1: What are your top three goals, what are two things you will need support to enact, and what is one area that is still confusing?

Standards
Science/CSTA/ELA/21st century skills

Small Steps
Students learn which codes are needed to move robots to their position at different points in the reception and ceremony.

Formative Assessment
Do now: What is something you are struggling with in coding your robot to move in the desired formation?

Standards
Science/ELA/21st century skills

Small Steps
Students practice coding as they move robots to and from various locations for the ceremony and reception.

Formative Assessment
Fist to five: How confident are you that your robots will move as planned at the event?
Exit ticket: (1) What is something a peer did that was outstanding? (2) What is something you did that surprised you about your work? (3) What is something you still need to learn more about?

Standards
Science/ELA/21st century skills

Small Steps
Students enact wedding of robots to demonstrate complex coding skills for fellow students, teachers, parents, and administrators.

Formative Assessment
Exit ticket: What made you most proud about your work today?

Summative Assessment
Bento box: Tell about a struggle and how you overcame it (social-emotional category); tell about three new skills you learned in this unit that you thought you wouldn't master and the steps you took to master those skills (cognitive category); tell how you were able to apply your knowledge in a way that differed from previous lessons, what was missing in it, or how you might like to do more of it in the future (physical category).

Standards
Science/ELA/21st century skills

FIGURE 3.3

Flexible Summative Assessment Models

• **Bento box:** Students choose from preselected categories among writing prompts, interviews with experts, short video clips with feedback, or even writing an alternative ending to a nonfiction event in a bento box.

• **Buffet:** Assessments have different weights, and students are free to choose any number of assessments that equal 100 percent. Students may select a mode (e.g., writing, speaking, drawing) that works best for them while fully demonstrating understanding.

• **Menus:** Similar to the bento box, students select one assessment from each of three categories (e.g., appetizer, main, dessert) where each category includes multiple modalities but requires students to address a specific aspect of learning. For instance, all the appetizers may ask students to distinguish between this math concept and a previously learned concept, with opportunities for multiple representations.

• **Tic-Tac-Toe:** Students must select three assessments, one from each square, to complete three across in any direction.

• **Bingo:** Students must select five assessments in a single row.

Developing metacognitive skills:

- What part of designing solutions was the most difficult?
- When you had difficulty, how did you seek help or support?
- What additional supports would have helped you be more successful?

Working with others:

- What is one way you think you communicated well during this learning?
- What is one way you think a peer communicated well during this learning?
- What is something a peer did that impressed you most during this learning?
- When did you have a conflict during this learning?
- How did you resolve that conflict?
- How would you wish to change your interactions with peers in the future?

Feedback for future:
- What is something you learned that was *surprising* to you?
- What is something you learned that you are still *curious* about?
- What is something you learned that is still *confusing* to you?

Primed to Activate

Using the tools in this chapter, you should be prepared to transform any lesson, unit, or curriculum into an experiential study that is student driven and teacher scaffolded. There will be hiccups along the way. These moments of growth are additional opportunities to demonstrate that learning is a process with multiple paths and continuous improvement. What matters most is that we keep moving forward together.

The following is a simplified list that may be helpful as you enact your design thinking work with students. There's no rigid structure but, instead, the list represents a synthesis of this chapter to help you support your learners as they follow their curiosity and co-construct learning alongside you.

- What opportunity for exploration embedded in your classroom is ripe for design thinking?
- How will you check for prior knowledge?
- How will you activate design thinking?
- What supports, resources, materials, or outside experiences would help students in understanding content and designing solutions?
- How are learning objectives reframed for the multiple pathways of designed solutions?
- What are the learning progressions toward your objectives?
- How will you know where students are in the learning progression?
- At what five spots in the learning process might you apply formative assessments to make learning visible and provide ongoing feedback?
- What summative assessment will allow students to use their own voice to demonstrate mastery of the content and hone their metacognitive skills through the design thinking process?

The iterative nature of design thinking means that as students work toward solving problems, their misconceptions are corrected through teacher observations and formative feedback. Whether they're calculating the area of a rectangle, unpacking the teachings of Confucius, or learning about the water cycle, students have rich opportunities to identify problems in the world that their knowledge can help solve.

– Notes from the Field –

The topic of scientific inquiry is a cornerstone of Catherine Croft's high school biology course at Fauquier High School in Warrenton, Virginia. Her dilemma? How to teach it in a way that would evoke passion and purpose in her learners. She identified the principal concepts embedded in the scientific method and quickly realized they aligned to the process of design thinking. For students to meet the standards of interpreting graphs to identify trends over time, distinguishing between independent and dependent variables, and conducting research, they would need to connect to content that would have an impact on their world.

Croft routinely enacts elements of design thinking in her classes. Through a series of brainstorming sessions, students identify an area of interest where they will focus their work, from video games to ballet to music to aviation. "Anchoring the learning to something my students are deeply vested in helps them see the value and impact of their work on the world around them," Croft shares.

Students must take the perspective of others who could benefit from a given designed solution. One student chose to conduct his research on the connection between violence and video games, hoping to open a window into his world and help others develop empathy for someone who feels connected through gaming. Another chose music, seeking to provide further evidence that young children benefit from music, which the student hoped might rally support for an expanded music program. After selecting their idea, students move into testing, which aligns with the element of prototyping. Finally, in the iteration and reflection stage, students identify aspects of their experiment that had an impact on their results.

Croft demonstrates that elements of design thinking can be readily applied in classrooms nationwide and can create more engaged learning. What's more, student choice in enacting the scientific method through their own design solutions has helped deepen student engagement and learning. Notes Croft, "By making the content meaningful to their lives and helping them see how it impacts their world, I don't need to seek buy-in. My kids arrive, ready to design!"

4
...

Understand and Empathize:
Stepping Back Before Stepping In

*I raise my voice not so that I can shout,
but so that those without a voice can be heard.*

Malala Yousafzai

When my son was in 3rd grade, he spent several weeks learning about circuits. The first batch of classwork came home in the form of prelabeled models that showed the flow of electricity, and students were asked to fill in blanks with terms from the model. Subsequent classwork asked students to recreate the diagram with blank spaces where labels and arrows once lived. Readily labeling wires, bulbs, cells, and arrows for current, my son returned to class confident in his understanding. In class, the students watched videos about how to construct circuits and observed as their teacher modeled the process. In groups, they were able to successfully construct their own circuits, which resulted in great joy and fanfare when one group was the first to complete a circuit that actually "worked."

On the day of the summative assessment, each student was asked to draw and then build the same model they had completed just days ago. My son could draw but not build the circuit. He was at a loss. Provided with the same materials from the same teacher in the same classroom where he'd demonstrated mastery just days before, he was unable to build a circuit. He couldn't articulate what part of the circuit was broken.

As an educator, cognitive scientist, and parent, I was stumped. How could a student understand a concept so well on paper, apply it in groups, and yet fail to replicate it on their own? Where was the misunderstanding? Was there a lack in fine motor skills or in cognitive ability? Was it anxiety?

How might the process of design thinking make learning more successful? It starts with helping students learn content—in this instance, how circuits give us electricity—through an understanding of how they can apply that knowledge to solve real-world problems.

Learning with Purpose: The Secret Sauce

Design thinking classrooms flip the paradigm of performance assessments at the end of instruction and, instead, posit the performance at the beginning. What's more, as co-creators of performance assessments, students identify problems that their content and their designs will help them solve.

Perhaps you've heard students echo statements similar to these:

- This person was alive 300 years ago, so why are we reading their journal now?
- This war was fought over a country that doesn't exist anymore, so how is this important now?
- I want to go into art or theater. When am I ever going to use an algorithm?

With every one of these utterances, students are asking, "Why is this content important? How can I apply this in the world around me?" The task here is to turn that question back to your students so they see understanding as a template for identifying problems and designing solutions for the things that matter most to them.

Regardless of the age of the learner or the content, teachers can launch into design thinking by providing a design challenge or scaffolding the organic development of a question based on the content. Older students, such as my teaching candidates at the college, have used theories of cognition to design novel classroom spaces that maximize collaboration and encourage community. But I've often been most inspired by my youngest students, who readily identify with characters in picture books, such as Kevin Henkes's

Chrysanthemum, in which someone is made fun of because she has a long name, and the students intuitively launch into their own design thinking projects, such as suggesting a new initiative to stop name-calling or create a friendship bench.

Although this may sound a bit like problem-based learning, there's an important distinction between the two: Problem-based learning asks students to "develop a viable solution to a *defined* problem" (Savery, 2015, p. 9), whereas design thinking refrains from defining problems for students and, instead, asks learners to seek out meaningful problems that their knowledge can solve. *Problem identification* is a key distinction between traditional pedagogies and design thinking, and it's one that supports our students in developing future-ready skills.

Laden with literacy, numeracy, social studies, and social-emotional skills, design thinking projects represent authentic, student-led, multimodal, and interdisciplinary learning where learners demonstrate higher-order thinking as they work to reimagine and actively redesign the world. Although a variety of scaffolds for support may be required, the iterative process enables students to return to any stage to extend or reengage with content until they feel confident in their ability to apply their knowledge in a meaningful way.

When Curiosity Drives Inquiry

The first element of design thinking is *understand and empathize.* As students engage with content, the guiding question is simply, *How does your understanding of _____ help you solve a problem in the world around you?* As you consider your own curriculum through the lens of design thinking, the driving question for you is this: *What is the big idea of this unit, and what do students need to know to demonstrate understanding?* Once you answer that question, you can repurpose your curriculum with students at the wheel.

Figure 4.1 shows questions, for both teachers and students, that get at the heart of understanding. Teachers will need to think about these questions as they're designing their lessons.

FIGURE 4.1

Teacher and Student Questions During *Understand*

Questions for Teachers	Questions for Students
What are the main objectives and standards that this lesson or unit meets?	What part of this content is most interesting to me? Why am I drawn to it?
What prior knowledge should students hold before tackling this content?	What prior knowledge do I have that is relevant to this content?
What knowledge should students be able to demonstrate to meet this objective?	What are the vocabulary words that I do and do not understand?
What tools, resources, or materials can I provide for students to use in understanding this objective? Do I need to provide 10-minute minilessons or learning walks?	What supports will I need to investigate the most interesting aspects of this content?
How much time can we spend learning this content? What multimodal activities can my students do within and beyond the classroom?	How have I seen this content in action? Where is it relevant in my life?
How does this content connect to issues students are most concerned about in their lives that they can address as they design solutions?	How can this knowledge help design a solution to improve the world around us?

Checking for Understanding: Teacher Questions

Formative assessments go hand in hand with understanding by making prior and current knowledge visible. The learning objectives and corresponding learning standards in your curriculum determine the types of preteaching you may be required to do and which content you can offer for student discovery.

Checking for prior knowledge through do-nows or check-ins ensures students are on the same page. Ongoing formative check-ins guide the materials you provide for students to deepen their understanding and support students' ability to find purpose in their learning.

Four goals in formative assessment apply to the element *understand:*

1. Check for prior knowledge ahead of current learning objectives.
2. Check for understanding of the current topic.
3. Identify student misconceptions.
4. Determine where students are in their learning and what supports you can provide to move them to their zone of proximal development (Vygotsky, 1978).

Before teaching high school science, Catherine Croft worked for nearly a decade in neurobiological research; after years in a research lab, she saw the utility of experiential learning. As a science teacher, she establishes foundational knowledge, or understanding, and helps her learners develop empathy for others through powerful yet playful experiences. She often introduces concepts through "mystery labs," where students come to understand material through exploration and guided discovery. Through a series of challenges, students compare water to rubbing alcohol and observe firsthand how water behaves in a special manner, leading to the concept of polarity. In this way, learners acquire accurate information in an applied and purposeful way.

Croft's school is home to many fine educators who make understanding and empathy engaging and meaningful. History teachers in Croft's building have used innovative methods for establishing foundational knowledge, such as introducing a historical figure through speed dating. This helps students learn about a range of historical figures before taking on more complex tasks, such as reimagining historical events from a different perspective or contrasting historical and current events.

The types of formative assessment you use during *understand* can vary depending on timing, style, and format (see Figure 4.2). You may need to gauge student understanding before starting class to see if the 10-minute minilesson is necessary. Or you may find it more important to collect formative feedback during the lesson as students pull out the ideas they find most important. Or you may wish to collect this information at the end of class to prepare for tomorrow's work. Ongoing check-ins are a source of constant support for students as they move forward in their learning. Be sure to keep the SMART model (Morrison, 2010) in mind as you develop assessments and provide feedback (see Figure 4.3).

FIGURE 4.2

Types of Formative Assessment During *Understand*

Timing	Before Class	**Check-ins and homework:** Use these to quickly assess what students know before instruction.
	During Class	**Concept maps:** Graphic representations of how concepts are related demonstrate how students connect knowledge to existing understandings. **KWL:** What do you know, what do you want to know, and what did you learn? Extensions include the following: Where will you go to seek additional information? How will that information help you? What aspects of this learning are most interesting to you? **Outlines:** Blank or prefilled outlines of content organize thinking and ensure understanding of key concepts.
	After Class	**Exit slips:** Responses to simple multiple-choice, true/false, or fill-in-the-blanks questions give a cursory view of ongoing learning. **3-2-1:** Three things I learned, two things I'm still confused about, one thing I'd like to learn more about. **Narrative prompts:** I used to think _____, but now I think _____.
Style	Traditional	**True/false:** This is a simple method of quickly determining understanding. **Matching:** Connecting terms to definitions demonstrates application. **Multiple choice:** If written correctly, multiple-choice questions are an ideal mode for identifying student misconceptions. What common areas confuse students, and how can you use that knowledge to create answer choices that demonstrate which students need additional support? **Fill in the blank:** These questions require retrieval with minimal prompting and demonstrate secure knowledge acquisition.
	Dynamic	**Sketchnotes:** Student notes can show images and corresponding keywords that help synthesize understanding. **Concept maps:** Adding to, revising, and changing concept maps over the course of the design thinking experience represent learners' shifts in understanding and show their evolving content knowledge. **Graphic organizers:** These are an ideal way to check for prior knowledge and see how students apply new understanding. **Categorizing:** Asking students to categorize vocabulary and then defend their categories in writing provides multimodal learning and supports interdisciplinary thinking. **Open-ended responses:** Asking students to list all their remaining questions about content, envision an alternative ending, answer a hypothetical question about content, or just complete a sentence demonstrates understanding and reinforces creativity and divergent thinking.

Format	Manipulative	Multimodal learning requires students to use a host of materials that may include the following: **Pencil and paper** to share their thinking. **Sticky notes or chart paper** to jot down ideas or wonderings. **Clay** or other malleable material to model understanding.
	Digital	Multimodal learning also requires students to demonstrate learning in novel ways: **Digital concept maps** can be used to revise and iterate their understanding. **Blogs** help learners keep a history of learning experiences, challenges, and opportunities. **Podcasts and YouTube videos** are dynamic ways of demonstrating knowledge.

FIGURE 4.3

Successful Use of Formative Assessments: A SMART Model

Specific	Feedback should be *specific*. What aspects of formative assessment were successful? What areas need additional support? For example, in U.S. history, do students need to better understand the differing perspectives of the Federalists and the Democratic-Republicans?
Measurable	Is there a *measurable* amount of content knowledge that students need to ensure they have adequate knowledge to take perspective and empathize? How many sources should they seek out, and what type of sources would best support their understanding?
Attainable	How *attainable* are the required supports? Have you already provided materials you can share with students? Do students need to plan a visit to the library during or after school? Are there resources they can access electronically on their own?
Relevant	How is this learning *relevant* to their lives? For example, do students make the connection between early events in U.S. history and their influence on the current structure of the country?
Timely	Is there a *time* limit for when the student needs to respond to the formative feedback to be prepared to continue in the design thinking process? How timely must *your* feedback be to ensure students can use the specific and measurable aspects of your feedback to move forward in *their* learning?

Based on the results of these assessments, you may wish to provide supplemental readings by adding primary or secondary sources to support learners studying history, plan an outing as either a field trip or a neighborhood walk to encourage local connections to science content, take a break from student-led understanding to do a minilesson that reinforces content essential for understanding, or have students participate in a fishbowl where they're asked to speak on behalf of multiple points of view. These formative experiences help prepare students to take on the role of the individual or systems that would benefit from a solution designed with their perspective in mind.

Whether the design challenge is for a single class period or the entire semester, students need to uncover how the content is relevant to their lives and what they can do with this knowledge to tackle a design project that will bring about change. In a 3rd grade classroom, students may be learning about water and what makes it safe and healthy for people to drink. A teacher would use formative assessment to measure the information students know about this topic before introducing the following design question: "How can you ensure that clean drinking water is provided for people in different environments, whether it be a rural village, a suburban neighborhood, or a big city?" Now students take the wheel in deciding which part of the content is most interesting to them and why. Groups often form on the basis of areas of interest, whereas individual designers may choose to tackle their own aspect of this learning.

Checking for Understanding: Student Self- and Peer Assessment

Paired with ongoing assessment, design thinking encourages students to identify what they understand, how their understanding is relevant to the world around them, and how they can leverage their knowledge to solve real-world problems. Simple yet meaningful self- and peer assessments collected throughout a well-planned design thinking project make student learning visible and enable students to take on much of the heavy lifting associated with qualitatively rich feedback typically provided by the teacher.

Framing self- and peer assessments as *thought partnerships* shows students how reflection, collaboration, and feedback strengthen understanding and fuel growth. Successfully observing yourself and others during each facet of the design thinking approach is an opportunity to highlight areas of strength and weakness. As students enact peer and self-reviews, they're learning essential skills of self-regulated learners and global citizens who can successfully collaborate with peers.

Students can conduct a *self-assessment* by looking at their understanding through three important lenses: metacognition, which refers to the ability to identify what you know and what you have yet to learn; self-regulated learning, in which you identify the skills you need for learning (Winne, 2017), such as how to use a graphic organizer or solicit feedback; and epistemology—your beliefs about knowledge that change as you move from more naïve to more complex understandings. Students can use the questions provided to assess their understanding in these three domains (see Figure 4.4).

FIGURE 4.4

Student Self-Assessment Questions During *Understand*

Metacognition: Knowing About Knowing	Self-Regulated Learning: Skills for Learning	Epistemological Beliefs: Beliefs About Knowledge
• What do I already know about this content? • What do I need to know to better understand this content? • What supports do I need to better understand this content? • Where can I get additional information about this content? • How will I know when I understand this content?	• What is my goal for learning this content? • How much time will I have to spend to better understand this content? • What strategies can I use to understand this content? • What strategies can I use to learn, remember, and apply information? • What strategies for learning would I like help strengthening?	• Is this knowledge certain, or is it likely to change? • Who constructed this knowledge, and what is their experience? • Is this knowledge connected to other areas I know about, or is it completely distinct? • How much evidence is there in support of this knowledge?

Peer assessments help students identify skills in their peers that can help them grow as learners (Hwang, Hung, & Chen, 2014). They're also an excellent precursor to teacher-driven formative assessments because they provide an opportunity for students to get feedback before submitting formal work. Using such assessments throughout the design process also fosters the collaboration and growth mindset that are essential for global citizens.

As students work together to understand content and identify a problem they wish to solve, not only do they learn that each person brings different perspectives to solving problems, but they also hone their skills of collaboration as they support one another in providing ways to move forward together. One model I've successfully used provides students with a learning objective and asks them to identify two areas of strength and two areas that could use strengthening for the peer whom they're reviewing (see Figure 4.5). For each area, students must share (1) something they liked about the way their peer demonstrated their understanding, (2) a question they had about their peer's understanding, (3) a suggestion for how to strengthen that understanding, and (4) something they learned from their peer.

From *Understand* to *Empathize*

Teachers consistently model empathy and the process of perspective taking for their students. If you use a getting-to-know-you activity at the beginning of the school year, bring it back later on and have students identify aspects that helped you gain a better understanding of them and that enabled you to take their perspectives.

What questions did you ask students to find out about their lives outside school? Did you ask about their caregivers? About the most difficult thing they've had to overcome? About the topic they loved most in school? About who helps them with homework? About their access to resources like the library? Students' responses help you gain empathy for each of your students. They also help in planning for specific learning and remaining mindful of the expectations you place on your students.

Perhaps you use preteaching tools to gauge student interest and understanding before teaching content areas. Calling on these tools to draw a direct connection between assessing student perspective and preparing for a unit of study will create a deeper sense of connection between the content and the students in your class. For example, before teaching about World War II, you might ask students to interview family members who may have served in the military. Or perhaps you might create a map of the world and have students label the countries in which their family members have lived. Modeling the way that you take perspective and develop a sense of empathy for your students establishes a framework for success.

FIGURE 4.5

Peer Assessment During *Understand*

Learning objective: _____ _____	I liked that... because...	A question I had...	One suggestion to become even stronger...	Something I learned from you was...
Areas of strength: _____ _____	I was so surprised by _____. I liked when _____. I loved that _____ because _____.	I wonder how _____. What if _____? Why did you _____? What are _____? How does _____?	One suggestion would be _____. Could you try _____? Instead of _____, did you consider _____?	The most inspiring part of your work was _____. Something you've inspired me to try is _____. Your strongest section was _____.
Opportunities for strengthening: _____ _____	I was so surprised by _____. I liked when _____. I loved that _____ because _____.	I wonder how _____ What if _____? Why did you _____? What are _____? How does _____?	One suggestion would be _____. Could you try _____? Instead of _____, did you consider _____?	The most inspiring part of your work was _____. Something you've inspired me to try is _____. Your strongest section was _____.

Building on a Strong Foundation

You've already laid the foundation for design thinking by supporting students in acquiring content knowledge and developing modes for collecting formative feedback to ensure students are progressing in their learning. The hallmark of design thinking is allowing your students to flex their wings and find ways to make that knowledge meaningful by solving important problems through considering perspectives other than their own. They can do this through the element of *empathize*.

Any content area or unit of instruction provides an opportunity for students to consider perspectives and develop empathy as they come up with questions to ask and problems to solve. You might ask 4th graders who are studying the three ways of changing light—by blocking, reflecting, or bending—how they might use one of these ways to solve a problem. What places may need more light, less light, or no light at all? For instance, how could students' understanding of light help them design a community garden?

Students must take on multiple perspectives to address this issue. They need to start by seeking out the purpose of the garden: Who would it serve? What are the community's needs in regards to the garden? What would make it successful in meeting those needs? Would the garden be used for growing food or decorative flowers? Given its placement, would the garden get too much or too little light? Answering these questions provides students with a perspective outside their own and sets the foundation for creating solutions. For sample questions in a variety of content areas, see Figure 4.6.

Empathy and Perspective Taking

Perspective taking is an essential topic of instruction across preK–12 classrooms. For example, in a 2nd grade author study, the goal of the unit may be to demonstrate how different characters perceive events. Second graders might take on the role of Fudge, the annoying little brother in Judy Blume's *Tales of a Fourth Grade Nothing,* and write a diary entry from his perspective. Some students may act out the scene where Fudge jumps off the jungle gym in an attempt to fly like a bird and breaks his front teeth; as Fudge, they must explain their reasoning and their feelings to his disappointed parents.

Perspective taking takes on a more complex role in high school. For instance, freshman students may be called on to defend or reject the statement that Franklin Delano Roosevelt's New Deal was an effective response to

FIGURE 4.6

Content-to-Question Connections

Domain	Content	Possible Student Questions
Elementary School	All about my neighborhood, social studies	How can we reduce our carbon footprint to keep our neighborhood green?
Middle School	Analyzing big data, math	How can we use big data to help explain and advocate for pay equity?
High School	Civics, government class	Can we develop a way to engage more citizens in our town?
Art	Street artists Basquiat, Haring, and Banksy	How can we use graffiti to improve a neighborhood?
Music	Different musical genres through the ages	How can we use music to bring about social change?
Theater	Theme of forgiveness in Shakespeare's *As You Like It*	Why was reconciliation successful in the play, and how might world leaders use these skills to solve major conflicts?
Physical Education	Resting heart rate	Can you develop a game that challenges people to lower their resting heart rate?
English Language Arts	Narrative writing	Can you create a campaign to combat bullying in schools using narrative writing?
World Languages	Conjugating verbs in Spanish, Italian, French, Latin	How can we create inclusive literature to encourage visitors to our town?
Math	Statistics or probabilities	How can probability help farmers predict the rainfall necessary for crop production?
Science	Classification and fungi	How can we use fungi to create environmentally conscious products?
Social Studies	Geography of colonial America	How does geography affect the economy of our town?

the Great Depression; they may be asked to write a persuasive paragraph in support of one of the initiatives to demonstrate their understanding. Integral to this learning is the identification of primary and secondary sources, knowledge of myriad issues of the time, and an understanding of the economic climate in the United States at that moment in history.

The role of the teacher in such activities is helping students build empathy for people affected by various events—that is, getting them to see things from another's point of view—whereas the role of the student is to view the content they've learned through somebody else's eyes. The essential question in the empathy stage is this: *Using my content knowledge, whose experiences would be improved by designing a solution?*

Checking for Empathy: Teacher Questions

The questions that guide students in empathizing with the people or systems whose problem they will try to solve will vary wildly. Some questions connect understanding to observation, such as, "How is the solution failing to meet the needs of the user?" Others connect empathy to current design, such as, "If someone has tried to make the fix and failed, why did it fail?" And others, finally, prepare students to generate possible designs in the ideation stage (see Figure 4.7).

As students work through these questions and broaden both understanding and empathy, how can the teacher assess this stage of the process? As students dive deeper into content knowledge and learn to take an alternate perspective, there are four goals for formative assessment. How well do students

- Connect content learning to identifying a problem to solve, one that is important to the learner?
- Research the issue and the perspective of someone affected by the issue to fully understand the problem?
- Study the current process in place to solve a problem by learning the history of the process and how it has changed over time?

- Use understanding, perspective, and knowledge of the existing solution to identify where the current fix is broken and enter the ideation stage prepared to generate ideas for problem solving?

FIGURE 4.7

Formative Assessment in Taking Perspective and Developing Empathy

Overarching Goals	Questions for Students
Teachers better understand their students when the students clarify…	What is something about the content we've learned that • You're still questioning? • Is really interesting to you? • Could make a meaningful change in the world? • Could help you solve a problem?
Students observe and take perspective of the individual or system affected by this content to understand…	For whom is this a problem? What are the different needs of the individuals/systems affected by this knowledge? Why is this a problem? What do I notice about this problem? What specific needs are not being met? How do you know these are truly needs? What evidence can you provide to support these statements? What solution is currently in place to address these needs? What do you notice about the way these needs are currently met? How is the solution failing to meet the needs of the user or system?
Studying current systems or processes, students strive to answer…	What specific aspects are broken or can be improved? Is it a small fix or a big fix? What do you notice about the current system, process, or item? Why hasn't someone made that big fix before? Has anyone tried? If someone has tried to make the fix and failed, why did they fail? What could you do differently?
Prepare to enter ideation, where students will seek to answer…	How can you use your understanding to design a new way of using this knowledge, an improved way of enacting this process, or a different design for an existing product that would improve the lives or experience of users?

The multimodal nature of design thinking enables students to document their progress in a variety of ways, using podcasts, collages, videos, blog posts, and so on (see Figure 4.8). When students have a choice in the mode of documentation, they develop a sense of the communications and representations that work best for them, preferences they might put to use in answering a design problem.

Checking for Empathy: Student Self- and Peer Assessment

Ongoing formative feedback during the element of *empathize* helps teachers identify how well students are applying content knowledge to identify and take the perspective of an individual or system for whom they're designing a solution. Student self-assessments ensure that the student is on the right track in terms of generating a problem to solve based on individual or system needs. Peer assessments ensure that student work is more polished before it's shared with the teacher, requiring less time on the teacher's part for providing technical feedback and more time to dive deep into the specifics of how students have connected their learning to solving a real-world problem. Framing these peer assessments as thought partnerships makes the process more powerful and ensures that peers see their role as supportive and not judgmental. Figure 4.9 provides assessment questions for students to consider during the element of *empathize.*

Design thinking is predicated on a student's ability to understand for empathy. Understanding may begin with a simple theorem in algebra, but it becomes more complex when students apply that theorem to build a bridge over a local stream or work with organizations such as Bridges to Prosperity to engineer footbridges in rural areas that create access to potable water. Applying the theorem requires developing empathy: For whom is access to potable water on the other side of a local stream a problem? Is there an existing solution and, if not, why? Understanding the theorem is deepened by meaningful application, in this case, the building of a bridge.

In *understand and empathize,* learners embark on their design thinking journey with a sense of purpose. Students ask, "How can I use this knowledge

FIGURE 4.8

Multimodal Formative Assessment During *Empathize*

Specific to empathy	Before class	Thinking of the person or system for whom you're designing a solution, • Write a letter from the perspective of the individual or system, stating their needs. • Create a checklist of needs of the individual or system, rank each need on a scale of 1-10, and sort needs into categories. • Take photos of current solutions and mark the areas in them that aren't taking the perspective of the individual or system. • Turn to a friend in a different design challenge group and talk about the reason you want to solve this problem.
	During class	Does your solution • Address the specific needs of the individual or system? • Address the most pressing needs? • Improve on a current solution? • Provide something meaningful for the individual or system?
Ongoing	Journaling or design notebooks	Journaling or design notebooks can span multiple subjects and are a tried-and-true space for students to reflect on their work, especially if they're encouraged to contemplate how they've solved problems in the past as a means to using successful methods in the future.
	Sketchnotes	By enabling users to add images to text, sketchnotes may help students recall key concepts or identify pain points they wish to solve in their design.
	Collages	Creating a collage of images that represent the systems, processes, or problems students wish to solve makes the problem visible. Building a living timeline of how this problem has been addressed fosters a sense of time, space, and the effort that has gone into previous iterations of designing solutions.
	Blogs	Keeping a blog throughout the design process provides a space for learners to reflect on their learning and see how their knowledge shifts throughout the experience. It's also a space to share with the wider community, where parents, educators, and others can celebrate the growth and development of each learner.
	Podcasts	Podcasts can be powerful in developing empathy. Students can use podcasts to interview specific individuals or those familiar with the processes they wish to improve.
Scaffolding toward ideation	Before ideation	In two minutes or less, explain the problem you wish to solve and why it's important to the individual or system—and why it's important to you.

to impact the world around me?" The fluid nature of design thinking enables learners to move through elements of design thinking based on need. That is, students may move from *understand and empathize* toward ideating potential design solutions, or they may bypass ideation altogether and move to modifying an existing solution through prototyping. The nonlinear process of design thinking is evident when a prototype fails and students must reconsider their idea or even rethink the perspective of the user or system for whom the solution was designed.

FIGURE 4.9

Student Self- and Peer Assessment Questions During *Empathize*

Student Self-Assessment	Student Peer Assessment
• What evidence do I have that this content can solve a problem of this individual or system? • How is my understanding of this content different from the understanding held by the individual or system in question? • What questions can I ask others to get their perspective on this content? • How clearly can I articulate how the content relates to the individual or system? • What aspects of my understanding will most help me meet the needs of the individual or system as I design a solution? • In what areas do I wish I had additional knowledge in order to take perspective? • How strong is the rationale I provided for solving this problem?	• What did a peer do or say that helped you see this content differently? • What are you still confused about after talking to your peer? • How will you change your process for working, thinking, or taking perspective after working with your peer today? • How might your peer take a different approach to connecting the content to the problem to be solved? • What did you learn from a peer that you'd like to try doing differently in the future? • What questions do you still have about your peer's work? • What additional evidence would help you better understand your peer's rationale for solving this problem?

Whether working independently or in groups, students are growing their competence as learners, their relatedness as classroom community members, and their autonomy in solving important problems. In the next element, *identify and research,* they will deepen their understanding of essential content while continually honing the crucial skills of divergent thinking and problem solving.

– Notes from the Field –

On one Friday afternoon, Laura Steinbrink watched as students in her 7th period mythology course counted down the minutes until the weekend—and then she had a brilliant idea. Steinbrink decided it was time to focus on the element of *understand and empathize* and place her students in the driver's seat. The challenge? How to engage learners at the end of the school day in learning content that is often rife with elaborate storylines, laden with jargon, and fraught with complex ancestry that affects the relationships of each character. The solution would have to help learners make sense of complex content and take the perspective of diverse characters, all while becoming more vested in their learning.

Steinbrink was inspired by a set of books authored by Zachary Hambry adapting lessons from classic myths to the lives of teens today. She decided to challenge her students to design their own mythological action figure based on a character they had studied in class. What's more, she asked students to include a marketing plan that explained how they might share the action figure with a target market; that is, the action figure would need to serve some purpose, provide a solution to a problem. This would push learners to take the perspective of another person, their target audience. To make it even more interesting, Steinbrink asked members of the school community to serve as judges at the culminating event, when all action figures would be on display.

The last period course on mythology was transformed into a buzzing workshop of research and problem solving. Students wondered how they could design an action figure that might be useful in the daily lives of a particular user while also representing one of the characters they had studied.

A lifelong learner, Steinbrink was inspired by educator Matt Miller, who envisioned a "caption this" activity, in which students add speech or thought bubbles to an image, to assess understanding. Building off this multimodal way to support learning, Steinbrink created a series of scaffolded activities to help learners practice taking perspective. One activity was a designed page with room for the character of inspiration on the left side and for a bitmoji of themselves (the student) on the right, with space for speech bubbles between the two. The students were tasked with giving advice to the character of inspiration to better understand the character's struggles and strengths.

One student was an avid outdoorsperson. She was looking at local businesses to see what tools people might need most outdoors, while conducting research about the places she might advertise her action figure. She knew that an important component of being outdoors is generating warmth and making food. She also knew that matches easily blow out in the wind. Taking the perspective of her potential customer and drawing inspiration from the Norse fire god Loki, she designed a creature who had the ability to withstand the elements and conjure fire for warmth. The judges and students were delighted to see that this action figure was also useful: Its head popped off to reveal a lighter for starting campfires.

The last period of the school day may be the most difficult time to enact sustained inquiry. Yet faced with a reticent group of learners, Steinbrink was able to do just that. "It was great to see the kids thinking about who would be interested in their action figure," Steinbrink shared. "One student was very savvy," she explained. "Knowing that an assistant principal judging the contest had a young daughter, she created a mermaid that was also a bath toy!" Students developed a sense of autonomy in choosing the characters on which they would model their action figures, competence in enacting their designs, and relatedness with their peers and the community by taking on the perspective of others and working to find ways to connect with those in the world around them.

5
...

Identify and Research:
Symptom or Root Cause?

Research is formalized curiosity.
It is poking and prying with a purpose.

Zora Neale Hurston

When Quest to Learn (Q2L) teacher Andrea Henkel presented the podcast project to her 7th graders in 2014, the prompt was simple: Interview a person in your life who was affected by 2012 Hurricane Sandy or by September 11, 2001. The podcast project was an extension of a unit on understanding and communicating narratives. The school, which is in New York and encompasses grades 6–12, is founded on the philosophy of systems thinking and design, as evidenced by the projects students engage in daily. The podcast project was ripe for cultivating understanding and empathy. Students would consider one of the two events proposed to understand the vastly different experiences of people whose lives were directly affected by those events.

The project was an intensive weeklong immersive experience, which Quest to Learn calls a Boss Level experience. Henkel's goal was to increase students' abilities to listen, talk to others, and synthesize their learning as they came to understand the lived experiences of others. Students interviewed a fellow New Yorker who recounted his experience overcoming a difficult time in his city's history. Others interviewed students and faculty at a school in the Rockaways that had been shut down after Hurricane Sandy. But then news broke about Eric Garner, a black man who died as a result of being held in a chokehold by a policeman during an arrest. Three students, one of whom actually knew one of Garner's children, felt passionate about digging into people's reactions to this event.

Garner's death sparked renewed anger, frustration, and fear in the minds of many New Yorkers. Although several students continued to focus on Hurricane Sandy and September 11, interviewing people who recalled losing their homes because of the storm or seeing posters of missing loved ones in the days after the terrorist attacks, those interviews took a backseat to the breathlessness and injustice these three students felt. Empowered by their new tools, these students worked to collect stories from their neighbors, relatives, and peers about the Garner event. The two original prompts were widened to include a third one, which addressed the root cause of the discomfort that many were feeling in the wake of Garner's death, a discomfort that would give new impetus to the nascent Black Lives Matter movement. Student interviews were cathartic for the interviewees and a deep learning experience for the student interviewers. They also helped students shed light on the distinction between symptoms and root causes of problems facing these learners and their community.

When You Don't Know, Ask

Although it seems natural to invite students to ask questions during the element of *identify and research*, what happens when they don't have questions to ask? Traditional models of education often focus on a single correct answer, so inviting students to ask questions and generate potential responses that may not be immediately "correct" may take time. However, once you've created a culture of trust and respect in the classroom, the layers of traditional models begin to fade away to reveal curious and inquisitive learners. When students no longer fear looking silly in front of their peers, they more easily share their divergent thoughts, questions, and potential solutions. And that's what successful learners need—to be able to use divergent thinking alongside the skills of research and evaluation.

Before designing solutions, students must identify the factors that affect their foundational question or problem. During *identify and research,* students distinguish between symptoms of a problem and the root cause, which has implications on the designed solution. Identifying causes can be guided by teacher, student, and peer questions and reflections.

Because the depth and breadth of projects vary, some might require the collaboration of disciplines or grade levels. In a multigrade study about land use, kindergartners and 8th graders paired up to identify a better use of land near their school. There was a barren space next to classrooms in the kindergarten wing. Nothing was growing there, and it seemed to be an opportunity to innovate. Students created sensors to determine how much light the area received and tested the soil to see what might grow in that space. Math, science, and history content came into play as students identified what was in the space before, how much space they had to work with, and how the makeup of the soil might affect potential plans.

The guiding question during *identify* is this: "What are potential causes of the issue that my design will help solve?" To guide learners in identifying the root cause, it's helpful to first ask them to restate the problem that their solution will address. For instance, the problem of water dripping from the ceiling on the living room carpet can be solved by either putting a pail underneath the leak or patching the ceiling. But it's only by addressing the root cause that you'll solve the underlying problem—that is, you must fix the issue that's *causing* the leak. To get at this information, learners will need to know where they can seek additional support, from community members to the public library to local organizations.

The following questions will help teachers scaffold student learning and can serve as ongoing formative assessment during this phase of the process:

- What question or problem statement will your knowledge of _____ (the content, skills, understanding) solve?
- How do you know that _____ (the content, skills, understanding) will help you design a solution to your question or problem statement?
  — What information do you have that will help you distinguish the root cause from symptoms?

— What information will you need to distinguish the root cause from symptoms?

• Where can you go to seek additional information about this problem?
— What resources might you need to better understand the causes of this problem?
— What tools might you use to better understand the causes of this problem?

• Whom do you know who may better understand the cause of this problem?
— How does this question or problem affect you personally?
— How does this question or problem affect someone you know in our classroom or community?
— How does this question or problem affect someone you've never met?

• What are all the reasons that make this a question or problem?

Problem Identification: Using Tools of the Trade

Searching for the root cause of a problem requires students to deepen their content knowledge as they explore each factor. Students must be able to translate learning into a question that is meaningful to them, identify aspects of the standards-based content that are ripe for design thinking, clarify their misconceptions, and synthesize content knowledge.

The tools used during problem identification are prime opportunities for formative assessment because they make student learning immediately visible. Graphic organizers are low-stakes ways to jump-start the process. These include Venn diagrams, storyboards, fishbone diagrams (see Figure 5.1), word webs (see Figure 5.2), KWL charts, concept maps, and sticky notes (see Figure 5.3). Graphic organizers also invite collaboration and discussion and don't require an exhaustive amount of writing before high-quality conversations emerge.

FIGURE 5.1

Problem Identification Fishbone

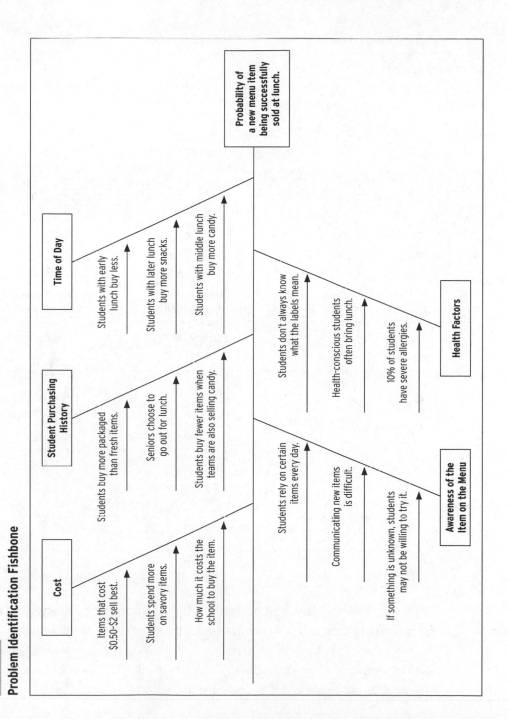

FIGURE 5.2

Problem Identification Web

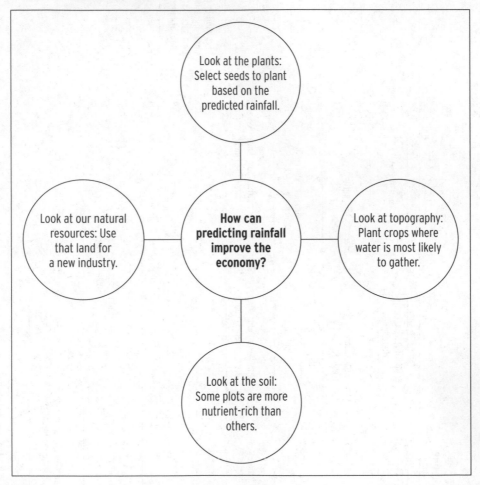

Look at the plants: Select seeds to plant based on the predicted rainfall.

Look at our natural resources: Use that land for a new industry.

How can predicting rainfall improve the economy?

Look at topography: Plant crops where water is most likely to gather.

Look at the soil: Some plots are more nutrient-rich than others.

Root problem identification can last for 10 minutes, a class period, or a full day, depending on the breadth and depth of the discussion. To begin, you might ask students to restate the problem in their own words and to generate as many causes of the problem as they can think of. Group brainstorming of potential problems is a great way to model the process of mind mapping because it helps learners find connections among their many seemingly disparate ideas. A whiteboard or chart paper on the wall provides an excellent canvas for students working in groups. Word webs or fishbone diagrams will jump-start ideas in individual students before they come together to identify all the potential culprits that might contribute to the problem their design will solve. In each instance, categories of contributors or causes will emerge. Figure 5.3 shows a whiteboard listing four potential problems that may be solved by predicting rainfall in a specific agrarian community.

FIGURE 5.3

Group Problem Identification on Whiteboard with Sticky Notes

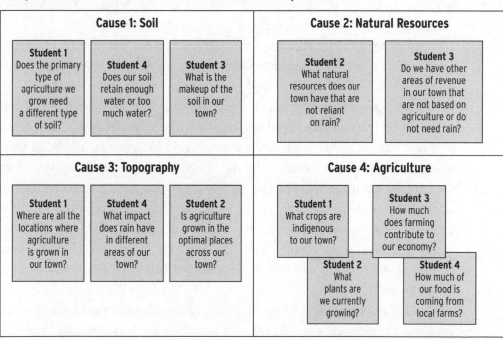

When first modeling the process of design thinking to students, these are some concrete ways to make the process visible and accessible, although you may find that students prefer to ask their own questions and generate their own list of potential contributing factors. Regardless of which tool you use, scaffolding problem identification in a multimodal way invites conversation, movement, and flexible thinking. Students are able to apply their interests and knowledge while expanding their cognitive toolbox of strategies for solving complex problems.

Real Work, Real Problems

Karen Schrier is associate professor/director of games at Marist College, where she teaches courses in design, research, and media. Her expertise in games, learning, ethics, empathy, and design helps her guide students through the design thinking process. Day one begins by helping her learners understand that good design is about good problem solving.

To create opportunities for her students to solve real-world problems, Schrier connects with community partners. For instance, one year she worked with Marist's Center for Civic Engagement to put out a call to organizations to submit a proposal defining a challenge they were facing that Schrier's students might have a crack at solving. Along with the problem statement, the proposal had to clarify who they are, who their audience is, and what their needs are. Schrier then invited the organizations to present in class so students could decide which ones to work with. Voting on six or seven organizations, the students were later placed in groups to design solutions for those organizations throughout the semester. Groups such as the Lucky Orphans Horse Rescue, the Salvation Army, the Franklin D. Roosevelt Presidential Library and Museum, and the Poughkeepsie Chamber of Commerce have been clients.

To support students in identifying and researching problems, Schrier guides them through a series of design exercises, such as *empathy mapping*, in which they use a simple visual to capture knowledge about a user's behaviors and attitudes. The goal is to deeply understand the audience of each specific organization. The features that emerge from the process help students understand what the designed solution must be able to provide.

For instance, a recent client, the Anti-Defamation League, presented the problem of how to reduce bias and hate speech online. Students researched the topic and ways to identify the root cause of the behavior before designing their solutions. Some students identified lack of education about bias as the root cause of the problem—that is, they believed that if educators had tools to support them in teaching about bias, it might help reduce hate speech and bias online. Other students identified the root cause as the individual's inability to recognize bias and hate speech online. After discussing various prototypes, the groups arrived at their own solutions. The group that believed that the root cause was educational ultimately designed teaching materials for school use, whereas the other group created a browser extension that would alert users when hate speech or bias was incorporated in web pages they visited or even in their posts on social media.

Checking for Understanding: Identifying the Root Cause

Once students document the many potential causes of their problem, they can begin to identify the likely root cause. Sample student and teacher questions can help isolate the root cause from mere symptoms (see Figure 5.4). Responses to these questions also serve as formative assessment and help guide research and the later elements of ideation, design, and reflection.

Identifying the root cause also has important connections to the domains of metacognition, self-regulation, and epistemological beliefs (see Figure 5.5). Metacognitive skills ensure that students know when they understand content and that they're prepared to ask questions to fill in gaps in their knowledge as part of a bigger problem-solving process (Schraw & Gutierrez, 2015). Self-regulated learning skills help students plan, monitor, and reflect on learning. Finally, students' epistemological beliefs enable them to see the interdisciplinary and evolutionary nature of knowledge and gain insight into the learning process that works best for them (Mega, Ronconi, & De Beni, 2014; Ozturk & Guven, 2016).

FIGURE 5.4

Teacher and Student Questions in *Identify*

Questions for Teachers	Questions for Students
Can the content you're covering be applied to solve the presented questions or problems?	Are each of the potential causes of your question or problem statement something that can be solved with your content knowledge?
What additional content pieces in your curriculum are connected to the presented questions or problems?	What other content knowledge can you draw from to help you identify causes of this problem or question?
How can you integrate additional content, processes, or information from your curriculum into this design experience to make the learning richer and include more of the curriculum?	How many causes for the problem have you identified?
How do students' questions or problem statements demonstrate misconceptions they hold about the content?	Which causes have less evidence of support?
Are there any topics that may need reteaching?	Which causes have more evidence of support?
How are students using evidence to support reasoning?	Is there any evidence of support that you think should hold more weight than others?
Are there students who have identified similar questions or problem statements?	Based on the evidence you've collected, what is likely the root cause (e.g., if you removed that cause, then your question or problem statement would not exist)?
Can students with similar questions or problem statements join forces to creatively design solutions?	What questions do you still have about the potential causes of your question or problem statement?
What supports will students need to research and support the evidence they cite for the problems they will solve?	What research will you do to determine which of the causes are root causes (e.g., if they were removed, then your question or problem statement would not exist)?

FIGURE 5.5

Student Self-Assessment Questions During *Identify*

Metacognition: Knowing About Knowing	Self-Regulated Learning: Skills for Learning	Epistemological Beliefs: Beliefs About Knowledge
• Where did you look when you needed additional information about this content? • How did you know this was a problem your learning could solve? • What are the needs of the user or system that this content will solve? • Now that you've documented your thinking, which of the causes do you believe is the root cause?	• How can you use graphic organizers to help understand information in a different content area? • What evidence did you use to support your identification of the root cause? • Where will you go to seek additional support to better understand the root cause? • What members of the classroom community might you consult or what tools might you use to conduct research on the root cause?	• Are the various causes of the problem similar or different? • Are there commonalities among the causes of the problems you've identified? • Are there other systems you can look to that have already tried to solve this problem? • How has your understanding of this content changed as a result of identifying a problem your knowledge will solve?

Peer Assessment During *Identify*

Regardless of whether students are working independently or in groups, this is a great time to introduce peer assessments so they can see how others have identified the root cause of their problem and gain a fresh perspective. The questions peers ask one another can help clarify misconceptions, deepen each student's thinking, and enable students to see—and maybe even get inspiration from—their peers' thinking process. These assessments elucidate how different learners can act as more knowledgeable others (Vygotsky, 1978) in modeling new ways of thinking about problems.

Peer assessments provide their most valuable feedback to the reviewee when scaffolded. Providing sentence starters ensures that peer assessments are qualitatively rich and more objective. Feedback sandwiches, in which students share two areas of strength that sandwich an area for growth, provide useful feedback to peers and enable them to practice being critical friends. Using Figure 5.6, students can select from each column, making sure to select different prompts for each part of the feedback.

FIGURE 5.6

Peer Assessment During *Identify*

To create feedback for growth, students share two *different* areas of strength surrounding one area for growth.

Feedback for Growth = ☀ + 🌳 + ☀

Area of Strength	Area for Growth
Our work on _____ in the classroom is clearly related to the problem you want to solve because _____ .	I would like to see if there is more evidence for _____ because _____ .
One way to connect the problem and its causes to the content we talked about in class is by _____ .	Something that could use more support is _____ because _____ .
The cause that seemed to be the best supported by evidence was _____ because _____ .	One question I still have is about _____ because _____ .
Something your problem identification work helped me understand better was _____ because _____ .	I wonder if you also considered that _____ could be a cause because _____ .

From *Identify* to *Research*

In problem identification, students isolate a single question or problem statement that their knowledge could help solve. Identifying the root cause of this problem can take on a life of its own. This nudges students into a new phase, *research*, a key skill that will empower students and enrich all areas of their lives. During this phase, students follow the guiding question "Which of our identified causes, if addressed, would solve the problem or improve lives, experiences, or process?" Students are now called on to leverage their interests and skills to identify which of the causes they've identified has the best evidence of support.

Teacher Questions During *Research*

Student work during the element of *research* provides valuable formative feedback for teachers. Inherent in the process are students' abilities to identify resources, synthesize knowledge, and reflect on their understanding. Paying careful attention at this stage will help teachers

- Evaluate if and when students may need to use teacher-provided supports to enhance their research.
- Discover how students use teacher-provided supports to deepen their understanding.
- Determine the strength of the rationale students use to substantiate their research.
- Identify how well students understand the concerns of the user or system affected by the problem.
- Observe how students collaborate with one another to identify and seek out supplemental material.

The amount of time needed to research questions will vary by student, content, and curricular constraints. Time spent researching doesn't determine the efficacy of the designed solution as much as perseverance and supports do. To improve access to the supports that students may need to facilitate deep learning, teachers may find it helpful to reflect on some of the questions shown in Figure 5.7 concerning the resources students use and the processes and practices they enact. Also shown in the figure are questions that students can reflect on to develop the perseverance they'll need to persist in this task.

Student Self-Assessment During *Research*

Figure 5.8 lists questions within the three categories of metacognition, self-regulated learning, and epistemological beliefs that students may ask themselves to stretch their abilities during the element of *research*. Students reinforce their skills across these three categories as they determine whether the sources they've cited are accurate and whether the information and data they've collected adequately answer their questions. Students see firsthand that knowledge is always growing and that they, too, have a role in growing and changing what we know about the world.

FIGURE 5.7

Teacher and Student Questions in *Research*

Questions for Teachers	Questions for Students
Are there research tools that need preteaching (e.g., how to do a Google search, how to identify accurate sources, how to use the library's catalogue, how to Skype a scientist)?	What research tools can I use to identify which of the possible causes will have the greatest impact?
Are students using the research tools to support their claims?	Is there research I can't do because I don't know how to do it or where to get this information?
Do students support their claims with well-founded research?	Can I support my claims with accurate research, data, and information? How do I know the data are accurate?
In conducting and documenting their research, is it clear that students understand the needs of the user or system?	How does my research relate to the needs of the user or system for which I'm going to design a solution?
Are students able to collaborate to solve problems and support one another in their work?	What are my strengths in research and which of my peers can I support with my research skills? Which peers might I work with to support my own research?

Peer Assessment During *Research*

Peer assessments during the element of *research* that provide scaffolded feedback prompts encourage students to learn from one another in a way that is low stakes and also may significantly affect the designed solution. Both

FIGURE 5.8

Student Self-Assessment Questions During *Research*

Metacognition: Knowing About Knowing	Self-Regulated Learning: Skills for Learning	Epistemological Beliefs: Beliefs About Knowledge
• How did I know when I had collected enough research on each potential cause? • How did I know that the rationale I provided was adequate? • How did I know if my sources were accurate? • How did I know if I needed additional support during research?	• How did I use research tools (e.g., computer, library, applications, interviews) to collect research? • How did I know which tools to use to collect research? • How did I determine if the research I collected was accurate? • How was I able to find other areas to support my research? • If I couldn't answer a question, where did I look for support? • What is something I did to collect research that makes me proud of my process? • How I can improve doing research next time?	• What did I learn about this content that I didn't know before? • What is something I knew about this content that I didn't know I knew before? • What is something surprising about this content? • What is one question from my research for which experts still don't have an answer? • What is one way I might contribute to answering this question?

peer and self-assessment questions vary, depending on the grouping of students. For instance, if students are working collaboratively, they might identify methods that their peers used that were helpful that they might like to try next time. When working independently, peer feedback provides students with ways to improve the research process, find a new way of looking at a problem, or ask a crucial question at just the right moment. Similarly, students may find that evaluating a peer's work helps them identify areas they might improve in their own research. Here are several prompts for students as they engage in peer assessment during this phase of the process:

• One cause that has great support from your research is _____ because _____.

- One cause that your research might better support is ___ because ___.
- Something you did/said that was really helpful in researching the root cause is ___ because ___.
- Something you did/said that may be more helpful in researching the root cause is ___ because ___.
- Something your research work helped me understand better was ___ because ___.
- An area where I think I could add something helpful is ___.
- **It's clear to me that your root cause is likely ___ because ___.**

Moving Forward with Evidence

Moving through the elements of design thinking in sequence can bring students closer to the content by engaging them in the development of innovative solutions to meaningful problems. The process of identifying and researching root causes can stand alone in supporting learners' ability to identify and research causes of any overarching question or problem statement connected to standards-based content.

Students who have well-founded support for the root cause are now prepared to move forward into the next element, *communicate to ideate,* where they'll collaborate to brainstorm opportunities to demonstrate their learning through designed solutions.

– Notes from the Field –

Vicki Lang was a 5th grade teacher in the College Community School District in Cedar Rapids, Iowa, when she was asked to take on a special assignment. Administrators in her forward-thinking district aspired to shift from a traditional grading system to a standards-based grading model. This new model would entail growth-centered practices that report snapshots showing a student's progress toward specific learning objectives. The administrators needed to design a solution to help the community understand this shift and accept the hiccups that might accompany implementation. Lang was tasked with working with a team of educators to design a framework and accompanying communications plan for sharing the shift to standards-based grading with teachers, parents, and the wider community. But first, she needed to understand the root cause of the anticipated concerns.

One of the most significant shifts in transitioning to standards-based grading is the way that student work is completed and expressed. Whereas traditional grading is based on tests, standards-based grading focuses on *mastery*, and scores are continually updated until the student has mastered the content. Because the goal is content mastery and not accumulating points, the role of homework also changes dramatically as it is no longer based on points. It serves, rather, as a demonstration of learning. It's where students *practice* their learning.

But some students may wonder why they need to complete homework at all if homework completion doesn't count toward their grade. "Students have to see how it supports their learning, or there's no motivation to do it," shared Lang. "And sometimes you don't assign homework at all—and that freaks parents and teachers out!" Once Lang and her team identified the problem—concerns about how student work would be completed and reported—they needed to understand the root cause of caregiver and educator hesitation so they could address those concerns.

But another concern soon emerged: Would students and their parents fully understand the new way in which student work was reported? Caregivers want to be able to help their kids, and kids want to be able to own their own learning. So, according to Lang, it became necessary to "translate the pedagogical language from the standards into laypersons' terms, helping caregivers and students understand the learning objectives—and this can feel like one more task on a teacher's busy plate."

Researching student and caregiver concerns around this transition helped Lang and her team understand the root cause of parental concerns, which was instrumental in designing their solution. Addressing homework concerns required revisiting the philosophical component underlying the new approach during every staff meeting or parent open house. Over time, all stakeholders understood and accepted the shift.

How to share student progress with learners and their caregivers was the toughest problem to solve. Because student progress is reported on a series of small goals, there's a lot more information to report. "It was hard to design tools that condensed so much information into progress trackers that were simple and quick for students to use. It went through a lot of iterations based on the kids' feedback," Lang explains. "Our kids are now so much more invested in learning for the sake of learning than I'd ever seen under traditional grading."

After researching caregiver and educator concerns about the shift to standards-based grading, Lang was able to use elements of the design thinking process to address the root cause of community concern: How do the grades reflect mastery? This process ensured that the district was able to move forward in implementing a complex shift in pedagogy with fidelity to their goal of demystifying student progress and supporting a growth mindset for all learners.

6

...

Communicate to Ideate:
Pulling Together to Design Innovative Solutions

The world as we have created it is a process of our thinking.
It cannot be changed without changing our thinking.

Albert Einstein

A common experience that launches design thinking projects is the marshmallow challenge. In this experience, learners are asked to collaborate to
design the tallest structure they can within a specific amount of time, often
only 10 minutes. Equipped with tape, toothpicks, string, and a marshmallow,
students or teachers embark on a messy and loud adventure to create their
structure. One fall, I tried a different version of the marshmallow challenge
in hopes of fostering a different conversation around ideation with my 2nd
grade students.

It was mid-November, and the preholiday jitters were in full effect.
Homework wasn't returning as regularly as scheduled, and the colder weather
meant more indoor recess, creating an even greater need for active learning.
I brought in a bunch of miscellaneous objects and asked students to work
in groups to create, in 10 minutes, the structure they would most like to live
in for a day. Straws, toothpicks, tape, yarn, licorice, playdough, and masking
tape were a few of the items I provided. There was only one rule: Students
could choose only two materials to build their structures.

Students chose various combinations of tools, from toothpicks and tape
to yarn and playdough, and quickly got to work. After 10 minutes, students
put their finishing touches on their structures and then took a gallery walk

to see what their peers had built. Groups took turns explaining their unique structure and why they would like to live there. Students were delighted to see all the dynamic creations, and they looked on in awe.

We connected the idea that each person has different tools unique to their experiences to the concrete materials, like straws and toothpicks. Then we talked about how the roles we take on in the classroom are also built from our experiences and can either stretch or stifle us. These differences define us, and we should acknowledge, honor, and support them to help us grow. The different structures were proof that we all have something unique to contribute and share. But it's when we work together that the magic happens. Are we all thinking about the problems flexibly? Are we all inviting different voices in developing these solutions?

With this exercise, I hoped students might be able to take the perspective of others and learn to consider how differences of opinion and different interests and abilities are also strengths and opportunities. In the element *communicate to ideate*, we invite learners to pull together to design innovative solutions.

From Many, One

The element *communicate to ideate* demonstrates the deep content knowledge that students have likely amassed as they've proceeded through the design thinking process. Here, they will continue to hone the soft skills that are so imperative for successful citizenship—skills in communication, problem solving, and divergent thinking. Such skills are also required to generate novel ways to solve problems. As students generate their solutions, teachers need to support them by helping them distinguish between simply hearing and truly listening, between simply seeing and truly understanding.

Scaffolded questions, supports, and reflections during ideation get at the foundation of a student's ability to truly listen. They also help demonstrate how well learners apply interdisciplinary content knowledge to come up with divergent solutions. What's more, as students reason their way through potential ideas using a variety of protocols as well as iterative feedback, they learn to be critical friends (Sussman, 2017).

From many ideas, only one can move to the prototype stage. The questions and check-ins provided to students in the *communicate to ideate* phase support their ability to self-regulate as they strategize and select the one idea that will move forward.

Adding Depth with Debate and Discussion

Because discussion, debate, and subjectivity play a role in the element *communicate to ideate*, so, too, does social-emotional learning (SEL). It's helpful to support student ideation with a framework that hones their social-emotional skills alongside their burgeoning interdisciplinary content knowledge.

Distinct from the first two elements of design thinking—*understand and empathize* and *identify and research*—*communicate* and *ideate* happen in tandem. As learners learn to articulate the solutions they'd like to develop, they're simultaneously ideating those very solutions. Two guiding questions ensure learners demonstrate respectful collaboration with peers at this stage of the process: (1) How do students communicate ideas for potential design solutions? and (2) how do students identify the best solution to prototype?

Various tools come into play at this point. Exit slips become an exercise in contrasting multiple potential solutions by weighing the pros and cons, and the KWL chart that students used during *understand and empathize* now provides support for scores of potential design solutions. The third element, *communicate to ideate,* continues to encourage a nonlinear path as learners produce a copious list of solutions.

Ready, Set, Ideate!

It's time to get out the multicolored sticky notes, pencils, and markers; it's time to start generating ideas! Clear off a space on desks, windows, and walls, or, if you're electronically inclined, open up a spreadsheet and let your creative juices flow.

If students are working in groups, they can each select a different color sticky note to keep track of and present their ideas. If using paper and tape, they can initial their papers to identify which ideas are theirs. The goal is not so much ownership of ideas as ensuring that each designer can speak to his or her ideas during communication.

Teacher prompts in the ideation stage are flexible. Here are some suggestions:

- Remember how the content is connected to your overarching question or problem statement.
- Recall how the lives of individuals or a system were affected by your overarching question or problem statement.
- Think back to your process of identifying the potential symptoms and the root cause of the problem.
- Call to mind the specific research that helped you identify the likely root cause.
- Now, if the sky's the limit, what could you design to address the root cause—to reduce, change, or eliminate it? No judgments. No limitations. Generate ideas, every idea you can think of, no matter how big or how small. Ready? Set? Go!

Teacher and Student Questions During *Communicate to Ideate*

Throughout the process of ideation, overarching questions addressed to both the student and teacher reinforce core concepts from the standards-based curriculum, where learning goals are clearly articulated and deepened through the iterative nature of questioning and ideation. Teacher and student questions make learning visible.

Overarching questions for **teachers** during *communicate to ideate* include the following:

- How do students determine the impact their prototype will have?
- How do students determine the amount of effort required to develop their prototype?
- How do students identify the solution they will prototype?
- Are the solutions directly connected to the root cause?

- What supports will students need to prototype their solution?
- What materials will students need to develop and test their prototype?
- What human supports can guide students as they develop their prototype?

And here are some overarching questions for **students:**

- Which solutions will have the most impact?
- Which solutions will require the most effort?
- Which solution will move to prototype?
- Does this solution directly address the root cause?
- What supports will I need from my teacher to develop this solution?
- What materials will I need to develop this solution?
- What community members might be able to help me in prototyping this solution?

Formative Assessment During *Communicate to Ideate*

During *communicate to ideate*, the potential solutions that students generate may include those that incrementally build on current models or exponentially shift the model itself. For instance, one high school history class studying voter turnout suggested novel ways to get more people to vote, offering an incremental solution to an existing framework. In contrast, another group of high school students suggested a complete overhaul to policy by pushing to lower the voter age. Although one solution is a more significant undertaking than the other, we can identify the potential impact of each through the process of ideation.

Science educator Heidi Bernasconi uses rapid ideation in her design thinking projects at Clarkstown North High School in New York state. After working with students to define a problem they wish to tackle, Bernasconi asks learners to fold a single sheet of paper in half three times, creating eight equal squares. She then gives her students one minute per square to quickly draw one potential solution for their problem. "I don't want them to fall in love with the solution," says Bernasconi as she walks around her marine biology classroom. "I want them to fall in love with the problem." By asking students to come up with many different solutions, she encourages them to stay open to new ideas and not get committed to just one. Once students have generated a range of solutions, from pie-in-the-sky to simple revisions of a current solution, she asks learners to collaborate in deciding which idea to prototype.

As students move through ideation, formative tools make learning visible. They will help you

- Assess how students apply standards-based content knowledge to ideate solutions.
- Determine what content students rely on in solving their problem.
- Identify students who can successfully communicate and resolve debates with peers as they select the idea that will move forward.
- Evaluate the rationale students provide for the design they select to bring to the prototype stage.

Student work during ideation is guided by two frameworks. First is a protocol for thoughtful discussion of the many potential design solutions, which helps equitably raise student voice (Fahey, 2011). Second is a matrix to help students identify solutions with the greatest potential impact (Fahey, 2011; Morin, 2017). Each framework provides rich opportunities for self- and peer feedback and offers insights into each student's learning.

Critical Friends Protocol

By this point, students have used their prior knowledge to generate a host of potential design solutions. Some students may choose to go through ideation independently; those working collaboratively will need support to ensure their ideas are heard and understood. For the latter, teachers can equitably raise student voice through a helpful protocol inspired by the critical friends group.

Critical friends groups are founded on trust and honesty, with the singular goal of providing valuable feedback for growth. Establishing a critical friends group among students may require clarifying that *critical* means essential feedback for growth, not criticism, and that feedback is truthful and constructive, a shared pursuit of improvement and growth.

Much of the work using critical friends protocols focuses on teachers as critical friends. Through this lens, educators work collaboratively to provide feedback, collaborate, and find solutions together as they create and grow their community (Bambino, 2002). Reframing questions as *wonderings* is helpful in asking for clarification. It may also be a powerful way to remove often innate deficit perspectives by reframing gaps in achievement with gaps in expectation (Chambers, 2009).

For instance, in a critical friends group I facilitated with teacher educators, one educator presented an issue with student behavior. Through conversations, thoughtful feedback, and questioning, what emerged was a question about the educator's perspective of the student. Together we realized that a deficit perspective was holding sway in the educator; the student's labeled learning difference was the focus and not the actual child. Using the critical friends protocol, the educators discussed ways to focus less on the label and more on the process of implementing skills to best meet the student's needs.

Using a critical friends framework may depersonalize questions so they're less about the individual educator or student and more about the practice. Modeling this type of feedback improves leadership and collaboration and can be a powerful framework in engaging students during communication. Not only is the ability to listen and offer feedback beneficial in continuous improvement, it's also aligned to the highest levels of thinking (Costa & Kallick, 1993).

Students may be apprehensive about being among the first to share their ideas, and they might prefer additional scaffolding to help decide who goes first. You might invite students to share their ideas in order of when their birthdays fall on the calendar. This may help speed up the process of deciding who shares their idea and when, and more quickly move students to communicating.

The protocol for this process is flexible. Think of the following steps as a guideline for creating the prompts that work best for your learners:

1. **Present ideas.** The *presenting student* shares his or her ideas (two to five minutes per student).

2. **Engage in thoughtful listening.** *Nonpresenting students* listen quietly and write down their thoughts or questions so they don't interrupt the presenting student.

3. **Ask clarifying questions.** When the student has finished presenting, *nonpresenting students* may ask a clarifying question. Clarifying questions are matter-of-fact questions—for example, "Why do you think we should put on the performance during the school day, as opposed to in the evening so our parents can attend?" They're not a judgment on the merit of the performance, such as "Performances are lame!"

4. **Present a response.** The *presenting student* responds to clarifying questions and revises the idea if they're so inclined. Presenters may use sentence starters to help guide the process of responding to questions, such as "If I understand the question correctly, you're asking if _____."

5. **Join ideas** (if collaborating in design). *Nonpresenting students* whose ideas are similar may offer to add their idea to that of the presenting student.

6. **Notice impact.** *Nonpresenting students* are now able to make "I notice" statements about the idea presented, with the following potential sentence starters:

   • I notice this solution is connected to the content _____ we learned in class because _____.

   • I notice this solution is connected to other ideas, such as _____ that we learned in class, or to an idea I considered when I was _____, because _____.

   • I think this solution may improve _____ for the people or systems that struggle with _____ problem because _____.

   • I think this solution addresses the root cause of _____ because _____.

   • I wonder if we could add _____ to this solution to address the root cause by _____.

The process continues until all students have shared their ideas. Students might now revise, improve, or extend their ideas using a SWOT analysis. By using the prompts below to consider the *s*trengths, *w*eaknesses, *o*pportunities, and *t*hreats of each design, students can alleviate potential weaknesses and increase strengths and opportunities:

- Are students able to identify areas of *strength* across shared ideas?
- Can students pull out the ideas that are *weaker* than others?
- Are students able to discern which ideas may offer *opportunities* for innovation?
- Can students foresee the *threats* of the design, how certain ideas may exacerbate problems or create new ones?

Following the critical friends protocol guides learners to have considerate conversations in which thoughts are respected and peers are encouraged to include evidence and reasoning in support of potential solutions. You might even ask students to consider other questions such as these: What content from our learning is this solution most connected to? What other content may be related to this solution? These teacher prompts support the work students do together as they share their ideas.

Over time, the process becomes second nature as students begin to use this language to ask clarifying questions and push their peers to think deeper about their shared learning. For example, one 4th grader observed a peer struggling with a microscope during an introduction to cell membranes. Instead of suggesting a solution or openly criticizing her peer, the girl asked, "I wonder if we could change the magnification to see more clearly?" This young design thinker invited her peer to be curious with her and see how, together, they could more clearly focus on the item on the slide.

A flexible protocol allows learner voices to be heard so every idea is given space. Such protocols also help scaffold potentially difficult conversations in the classroom. By honing the critical skills of listening before speaking and asking for clarification before making conclusions, students become clearer and more thoughtful communicators.

The Action Priority Matrix

After generating a multitude of design solutions, students now evaluate and categorize solutions based on their potential impact and the level of effort they might require. A reenvisioned action priority matrix (Morin, 2017) can help by making learning visible (see Figure 6.1). One axis in the matrix represents the level of impact; the other represents the level of effort. Students are asked to consider how much of an impact a solution will have, as well as how much effort it will take to enact it. Students place their ideas in the corresponding quadrant in the matrix and consider whether they can improve or revise the idea. Once completed, the matrix provides a strong visual representation of solutions that are most viable and that should move to prototype.

FIGURE 6.1

An Action Priority Matrix for Categorizing Solutions

EFFORT		
+	**More Work Than Working** Considerations: How much time will it take to get this idea started? How much will this idea remove, lessen, or change the root cause? Is there a simpler way to get at the same outcome?	**Big Opportunities** Considerations: How much outside support will you need? How long will it take to see this project through? When will you know if this opportunity has paid off?
−	**Why Try?s** Considerations: Can this idea be made more impactful?	**Quick Wins** Considerations: What supports do you have in place already? How can you work within your community to quickly build this solution? When will you know if this is a quick win?
	− IMPACT +	

As learners go through this exercise, they must consider how much support it would take to begin a given project or what supports are already in place to get this idea off the ground. They must also consider how much of an impact each idea might have on the audience it's intended to serve. As science teacher Heidi Bernasconi noted, "The sweet spot is where the idea has maximum impact and moderate effort. When my students look at the ideas they've generated and assign them to one of these four quadrants, it's another assessment for me to see if they truly understood the perspective of the end user, and if they're designing a solution that will truly impact the end users' lives for the better."

Student Self- and Peer Assessment During *Communicate to Ideate*

Using the ideation protocol based on the critical friends group provides ample opportunity for students to collaborate and communicate. The matrix for categorizing the opportunities and effort required for each idea is yet another occasion for students to reinforce learning and build knowledge. In this stage of the process, self- and peer assessments can help students reflect on their learning, provide formative feedback, and suggest supports they may need moving forward.

Student Self-Assessment

Providing self-assessment questions in a menu format is a quick way to collect student feedback in a few minutes at the end of class (see Figure 6.2). Students can select one question to answer from each column to ensure they're reflecting on their knowledge (metacognition), their skills (self-regulated learning), and their beliefs (epistemology). New digital tools like FlipGrid or SeeSaw instantly document student responses alongside reflections that journal student growth over time.

FIGURE 6.2

Student Self-Assessment Questions During *Communicate to Ideate*

Metacognition: Knowing About Knowing	Self-Regulated Learning: Skills for Learning	Epistemological Beliefs: Beliefs About Knowledge
• How did your knowledge help identify possible solutions? • What information do you wish you had during ideation and communication? • How strong are the rationales you provided for your ideas? • How will you know if your idea helps solve the problem?	• What is one way you knew you were successful in communicating during ideation? • What is one way you could be more successful in communicating next time? • How well did you listen to and respect your peers during this process? • What is something you would change next time?	• How did a peer's approach to this information differ from your thinking? • What was something that took a while to understand? • What was something that was difficult to understand initially that became clearer as you talked with your peers? • Can you explain how many of the ideas suggested could help solve this problem?

Peer Assessment

Peer assessments during *communicate to ideate* give students the opportunity to support and encourage one another with scaffolded prompts. These prompts can solicit feedback about how a peer demonstrated strong listening skills, modeled critical thinking abilities, or provided good feedback for growth and ways to improve. Because the focus in ideation is largely on divergent thinking and communication, feedback focuses on soft skills that will serve learners well as they cultivate friendships and work collaboratively in the future.

Students may wish to provide feedback to a peer using a feedback sandwich (an area of strength, an opportunity for growth, an area of strength), in which case they can select three sentences to complete from Figure 6.3. However, if students are working in groups of four or five, it may be useful for students to provide one opportunity for growth and one area of strength for each peer in their group.

FIGURE 6.3

Peer-Assessment During *Communicate to Ideate*

To create feedback for growth, students share two different areas of strength surrounding one area for growth.

Feedback for Growth = + +

Area of Strength	Area for Growth
Something _____ did to demonstrate they really heard and understood my idea was _____.	Something _____ did or said that wasn't helpful was _____ because _____.
Something _____ did to show they clearly understood the rationale I provided for one of the ideas was _____.	One way _____ could have improved the iteration process would have been to _____.
Something _____ did or said that I most admired during the ideation stage was _____.	Something _____ might have done differently during iteration was _____.

Innovating Through Ideation

During *communicate to ideate*, students generate potential solutions demonstrating content knowledge aligned to standards-based learning. But perhaps more important, students are making connections between what they're learning in your class *currently* and what they've learned *previously*, making connections to what they're currently learning in *other* classes, and getting a glimpse into their *future* learning experiences. What's more, as students are asked to communicate their ideas, they're reinforcing knowledge by explaining and often teaching their peers. In becoming Vygotsky's (1978) "more knowledgeable other," students are growing competence and efficacy.

The teacher and student questions posed during ideation (see Figure 6.4) move beyond ones that simply identify quickest wins for prototyping. Responses show how the process has enhanced and reignited your curriculum. Ideation opens up a world of opportunity to celebrate the deep work happening in your classroom and bring in the wider community to help enact meaningful change.

FIGURE 6.4

Considerations for Teachers During *Ideate*

Ideation invites questions such as	Answers invite ideation about
How are students deepening their understanding of standards-based core content?	What additional modalities can be used to assess for mastery of this content?
What new content are students learning through these elements?	What standards-based content does this learning meet that didn't previously live in this unit of instruction?
Are students learning content that typically lives in a different unit during the course of your semester or year?	How can the subsequent unit be revised so students use their current learning to dive more deeply into that unit?
Are students learning content that typically lives in different content areas?	Is there a colleague working with those students with whom you might collaborate to demonstrate the interdisciplinary aspects of this learning and deepen student engagement across the curriculum?
Are students learning content that may have an impact on their previous learning?	Is there a colleague working with those younger students with whom you might collaborate so your students can use their knowledge to work with, inspire, and support younger students?
Is the content that students will be learning offered in a class they'll be taking in the future?	Is there a colleague working with older students with whom you might collaborate so older students could inspire, support, and provide feedback for your students?

– Notes from the Field –

Middle school science teachers Rebecca Henderson and Mark Davis were independently engaging in design thinking projects in their classrooms when they discovered an opportunity to ideate across classrooms. As a robotics teacher, Rebecca Henderson readily applies elements of design thinking to help her students use their knowledge to solve problems in the classroom. Mark Davis encourages students to use elements of design thinking as they apply skills from his course on digital literacy to find solutions that emphasize the 4Cs of collaboration, communication, critical thinking, and creativity.

During a professional development session, Davis and Henderson shared their current classroom work with colleagues and identified an overlap in their curriculum. Both educators were teaching the 4Cs; Henderson was teaching them through robotics, and Davis was teaching them through digital literacy (see Figure 6.5). This provided an opportunity for their students to collaborate to learn new skills while providing feedback to one another. As educators, Davis and Henderson knew that the best way to demonstrate knowledge acquisition is to explain it to someone else, and their thought partnership was forged.

Groups from each class took turns presenting to peers in the other class. The goal was to teach a concept they had learned in their class to a novice. Students provided self- and peer assessment in addition to the feedback provided by class teachers. Students took this feedback back to their classrooms, where they continued in their design thinking work with a deeper understanding of their content and a more focused path forward in their work. This process helped demonstrate that students had acquired knowledge aligned to the standards-based curriculum. It also went beyond content by honing the soft skills of collaboration, communication, critical thinking, and creativity.

FIGURE 6.5

Teams Henderson and Davis: Collaborating on Content

	Team Henderson	**Team Davis**
Content	Coding EV3/NXT robots, 3D print design, evidence diary	Coding in JavaScript, problem-solving process, design thinking
4Cs	Practicing skills to function as a responsible team member; reinforcing communication, collaboration, critical thinking, and creativity	Recording reflections and team building through clear communication and creative problem solving
Interdisciplinary Connections	Programing robots to complete challenges; informational writing; BlocksCAD 3D software to map coordinates, resulting in a final printed object	Virtual reality front-loaded research (social sciences); simple physics lesson (science); informational writing (English language arts)
Standards	ET2.1 (5-8) Utilize the attributes of a design process to solve a real-world problem. ET2.3 (5-8) Utilize processes (i.e., research and development, invention and innovation, experimentation and troubleshooting) in designs that use criteria and constraints, leading to useful products and systems.	CSTA: 2-AP-12 Design and iteratively develop programs that combine control structures, including nested loops and compound conditionals. (P5.1, P5.2) CSTA: 2-AP-17 Systematically test and refine programs using a range of test cases. (P6.1)

7

· · ·

Prototype and Test: The Messy Path Forward

We learn from failure, not from success!

Bram Stoker, *Dracula*

Author studies are a common way for elementary schools to engage in a thematic or shared curriculum. One Title 1 public school in New York City chose to do an author study on renowned children's author Ezra Jack Keats. Teaching artists Jody Drezner Alperin and Vicky Finney Crouch worked with students in a K–2 self-contained 12:1 classroom to explore and breathe life into Keats's texts around the topics of compassion, differences, resourcefulness, and city life. Recreating the experiences of characters in Keats's book *Pet Show!* enabled learners to take the perspective of the missing pet and his resourceful owner.

While reading the book, the children became curious about other animals people keep as pets. Driven by that curiosity, the children and teachers took a field trip to a local animal rescue to meet some of the pets that were looking for a home and to learn about the work required in caring for a pet. Students noticed that the rescue seemed to be in need of support. One child wanted to know the kinds of supplies required to take care of animals. The animal rescue shared their list of needed supplies, and the children eagerly headed back to school with a plan: They would collect the needed materials for the homeless animals to donate to the rescue.

The children decided to conduct a drive, but they needed to find a way to communicate their need to the school and community. Supported by their teacher, the students asked the principal if they could announce their drive over the loudspeaker and if they could write letters to the community requesting supplies and send the letters home with all the students by placing them in the students' backpacks. The answer was a resounding *yes!* The community responded to the call, and soon materials flowed to the school for the rescue animals. The children felt empowered knowing they could communicate with the community and other classrooms throughout the school.

The two teaching artists next decided to share Keats's book *A Letter to Amy* through song and play-acting. Inspiration struck as the children watched Peter walk to the mailbox to mail his birthday party invitation to Amy. Connecting this to their own lives, the children wondered if *they* could create a mail system in the school to communicate with other classrooms. The children in that K–2 self-contained classroom weren't strangers to feelings of isolation and were hopeful they could encourage other classrooms to join in their mail system. Not only would they be able to communicate the needs of the rescued animals, but they'd also build a bridge between their classroom and the rest of the school. When nine classrooms eagerly agreed, it was time to build a prototype of their mail system.

Through their research, learners knew they would need mailboxes. But the blue city mailboxes they were familiar with gave no indication of what items were to be picked up and what items should be delivered. Supported by their teachers, the children learned that some mailboxes use flags to indicate when mail is ready for pickup—and soon flags were on each mailbox in the school! But it was still unclear who would write letters and when the students would regularly pick up the mail.

Through iteration and testing, the students found a pickup time that worked best, and they invited whole classrooms as well as individual students to write letters. They also began using the mail system to communicate about more than just the needs of the animal rescue. Soon students were writing letters to learners in other classrooms to share their knowledge of the life and experiences of Ezra Jack Keats. They were delighted to learn that he began as an illustrator before becoming an author. As emergent writers and readers, the children were thrilled to think about their own creative work of illustrating or shaping words appearing on the pages of a book.

Student learning in this instance went beyond content and theme to include the skills of listening for understanding to identify the needs of the shelter animals and then collaborating for action to collect the needed items. In the process of building that one solution, students solved an even more profound problem—how to break through the boundaries of the four walls that often kept them separate from the rest of the school.

You Have to Crack a Few Eggs…

The beauty in reframing education through the lens of design thinking is not simply in the interdisciplinary approach to learning content, or in the applied manner in which educators and students design solutions to meaningful problems, or in the impact of working passionately toward a goal that fuels a sense of purpose. The true magic lies in the way it *retrains* each of us to look at snafus not as an end point but rather as an opportunity to stop, think, revise, and rework our solutions.

Notice that the word *fail* doesn't appear in that last sentence. The finality of failure is removed in elements of design thinking. There's no single summative assessment from which a learner can't rebound. Instead, consistent opportunities for improvement, revision, and reflection help students know *when* they know something. And in the process, they come to see themselves as builders of knowledge.

While learners flex their divergent thinking muscles to consider multiple ways of addressing the root causes of various problems, their critical-thinking skills will ensure they're prepared for the next element in the process—*prototype and test*—where they'll enact their ideas.

Guiding Questions During *Prototype*

Students arrive at the element of *prototype and test* with an idea in place. In the prototype part of the element, learners engage in higher-order thinking to answer the guiding question "What resources or materials must I use to design this solution?" These resources may include lines of poetry, songs from an artist, LEGO bricks, or 8-foot-long 2x4s. What's key is to just get started!

According to education experts Alyssa Gallagher and Kami Thordarson (2018), "prototyping can help alleviate analysis paralysis!" (p. 128). Instead of perseverating on which solution to use moving forward, students select the best idea they can come up with and realize that any necessary changes will become clear as they move forward in designing their solution. As they test the success of that solution, noticing what worked, what didn't, and how they might pivot in the future, they're also generating rich examples of content knowledge applied to solve novel problems. In addition, the way in which learners seek support demonstrates autonomy, fostering both a sense of competence and relatedness to others in the classroom and wider community.

Student and Teacher Questions During *Prototype*

As students design their solutions, the formative assessment goal largely focuses on the supports and materials necessary to create a successful prototype. Access to materials and resources can be limited, so it's a great opportunity to reflect on how learners might find these supports in their communities. The supports are not so much founded on financial support as they are on knowing the right questions to ask and identifying educators, parents, or community members who may help answer those questions. If the purpose of education is to create a more informed citizenry, there's no better way to build this knowledge than by demonstrating our reliance on one another to strengthen and support our shared work.

Students can be primed to consider specific questions as they engage in prototyping. These questions can be posed as a do now or an exit ticket, depending on the goal. Similarly, teacher questions during prototype help prepare you to best support your learners by anticipating their needs and ensuring that you're ready to pivot with them as they interact with the content on a deeper level.

Overarching questions for **students** during *prototype* include the following:

• How does my content knowledge help me design the best possible prototype?

- What resources do I need to design this solution, and how will I gather them?
- How can I clearly communicate my thoughts and needs while prototyping?
- How will I ensure that my peers are also able to share their thoughts while prototyping?
- If my prototyped solution is successful, how will I know?

Similarly, here are some overarching questions for **teachers** to consider:

- How are students using the content knowledge in designing their prototype?
- What resources, materials, and access to experts can I provide to support my learners?
- How are students accessing and using materials as they design their solution?
- How well do students communicate as they design their solution?
- What concepts aligned to the intended curriculum are addressed by the prototype?
- What additional concepts not previously aligned to the curriculum are addressed by the prototype and provide practice using skills essential to 21st century learners?

Formative Assessment During *Prototype*

Prototyping is about more than just how students acquire resources. It's about demonstrating how students use their current knowledge to stretch their understanding and become an expert in their domain. As students create their prototype, whether a stage play on sustainability or devising a better route to get to school in the morning, there are rich opportunities for formative feedback that will help you

- Identify where students are in their learning progression toward mastery while developing a prototype.

- Explore those concepts that are especially captivating to learners, including new ways of looking at content.
- Identify concepts that students struggle with as areas for additional support.
- Determine which topics students rely on most when applying their knowledge toward designing a solution.
- Document different student voices present in the creation of each solution.
- Demonstrate how students perceive the prototype and their content knowledge as benefitting a specific system or individual.

Student Self-Assessment During *Prototype*

Design thinking is human-centered design, which is why educators are the ultimate design thinkers. The prototypes of *our* designed solutions, otherwise known as lessons, experiments, field trips, and projects, can serve as templates for supporting our students as they prototype and, later on, implement their designed solutions.

Gathering ideas, resources, materials, and information during prototyping is an exciting process. It's also rife with questions, comments, concerns, and potential conflicts, so it's an ideal time to support students in developing successful social-emotional skills. It's also rich in opportunity to provide feedback on both content and process. For instance, how well are students successfully engaged with peers in debate around the designed solution? How well are students applying their knowledge in their designs? How successful are students at clarifying their expectations of their prototype?

Using our toolbox of strategies, we can hone students' metacognitive and self-regulated skills, while pushing them to think deeply about their epistemological beliefs and the social-emotional skills they'll need to successfully navigate challenging situations (see Figure 7.1). Students' self-assessment can take place at any point during prototyping; certain questions may apply to individual students, or they may be asked of all students, depending on the need and opportunity. Each question reinforces successful problem-solving

FIGURE 7.1

Student Self-Assessment Questions During *Prototype*

Type of Knowledge	Questions for Student Self-Assessment
Metacognition: Knowing About Knowing	• What information (content) was most useful in designing a solution? • What information was previously missing but was learned while designing the solution/prototype? • How will you know if the designed solution is successful? • Who will try the designed solution to tell if it's successful? • What specific behavior will you look for to see if the design works? • What specific outcomes will you look for to see if the design works?
Self-Regulated Learning: Skills for Learning	• What problem-solving strategy was most helpful in creating the prototype? • When was a time you were stuck? • When did you know it was time to get support? • How did you get support when stuck? • What is a strategy you used to design the solution that you would like to try again? • What is a strategy you used that you would like to do differently next time?
Epistemological Beliefs: Beliefs About Knowledge	• What part of prototyping took longer than you expected? Why did you initially think it would be quicker to complete? • How many different ways did you consider designing your solution? • How did a disagreement improve the designed solution? • How did it feel to work on a design with no instructions? • When did you feel especially proud of your work?
Social-Emotional Learning	• Was there a time when you didn't agree with your peers? If you were able to resolve the debate, how did you resolve it? • What is one area in which you'd like support in working with your peers in the future? • What is an area where you felt particularly strong in working with your peers? • Can you name a few peers who surprised you during prototyping? How did they surprise you? • What is one way you felt *heard* in designing your prototype? What is one way you did *not* feel heard? • Which of your peers was heard most during prototyping? Which of your peers was heard least?

strategies by asking learners to consider multiple perspectives while also challenging their knowledge beliefs and making their thinking clear.

Peer Assessment During *Prototype*

Peer assessment is useful not only in providing low-stakes feedback to learners, but also in strengthening student work and students' relationships with one another. In a classroom with a culture of collaboration and mutual respect, peer assessments are a powerful way to increase learning and invite every student into a conversation about learning and growing together.

Providing critical but warm feedback is particularly important during *prototype*. The feedback sandwich approach is useful here. So, too, is encouraging learners to be specific with their feedback, ensuring that their comments and critiques address specific attributes of the designed solution. That way, the recipient of the feedback knows exactly how to move forward, and the provider of the feedback develops a sense of efficacy in learning how to ask questions in a thoughtful yet productive way that concretely improves a peer's outcome.

The overarching goal of peer assessment during *prototype* is for students to explain to one another (1) what they hope their design will solve; (2) how they created the prototype from content knowledge; (3) how they'll collect information to validate or improve their design; and (4) something that might improve the design or shift their thinking about the designed solution. The template in Figure 7.2 helps ensure that everyone receives rich feedback.

There are many ways to easily provide peer assessment through digital tools, from a simple Google Form, to SeeSaw, VoiceThread, FlipGrid, or Peergrade, depending on the age and interests of the learners. As students prepare to share written, visual, or audio evidence of their designed solution, they should accompany that evidence with an explanation of the content that inspired the prototype, how the prototype solves a problem, how they'll test the prototype, and something they're still working on.

FIGURE 7.2

Peer Assessment During *Prototype*

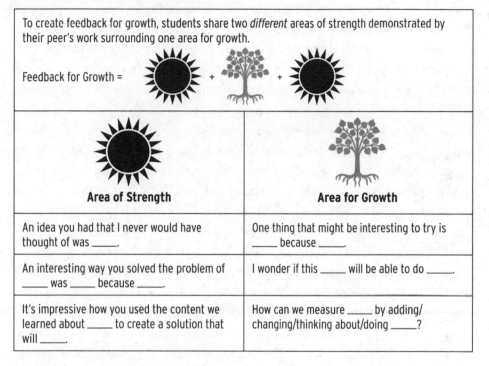

To create feedback for growth, students share two *different* areas of strength demonstrated by their peer's work surrounding one area for growth.

Feedback for Growth =

Area of Strength	Area for Growth
An idea you had that I never would have thought of was ____.	One thing that might be interesting to try is ____ because ____.
An interesting way you solved the problem of ____ was ____ because ____.	I wonder if this ____ will be able to do ____.
It's impressive how you used the content we learned about ____ to create a solution that will ____.	How can we measure ____ by adding/changing/thinking about/doing ____?

From Prototype to Test

A parent approached me recently to share the story of a fascinating design thinking project at her son's school. The school was putting a renewed emphasis on social-emotional development, and students were asked to think of something that causes them stress in their daily lives. They were asked to identify what they believed was the root cause of that stress and create a prototype or design a solution to help assuage it. It was an affluent district, so most students didn't point to scarcity of resources but rather to scarcity of time and the tremendous pressure that caused.

One student in particular was anxious about consistently arriving late to school. Parents were responsible for bringing their children to school on time, so there was no bus company to call or route to improve for a more timely arrival. Through research and discussion, the student decided that the root cause of the problem was the time he was waking up and that perhaps waking up earlier would help. But how long should he experiment with this new behavior, and how much data would he need to collect to support or reject this designed solution? In the element *test,* we'll see how he discovered the optimal solution for this problem of persistent tardiness, allaying anxiety and increasing his efficacy in solving real issues.

If the guiding question for *prototype* centers on resources for design, the guiding question for *test* moves to measuring the utility or impact of the prototype. Supporting learners during their test requires clear assessment questions such as "How will you know if the solution is successful? What behaviors, understandings, or feelings might change to show that this solution is working? How much time might you need to see an impact?"

Designed solutions may be tested in 10 minutes or 10 days. What's important is what the student does if the prototype fails to solve the problem during the test. The student working to solve the issue of tardiness required multiple points in time to decide whether his solution would work.

As you prepare students to test their designed solutions or prototypes, this is a natural place to connect their content to the nature of scientific inquiry. Testing is an invitation into a discussion on independent and dependent variables and a great primer for students to understand ideas of validity and reliability in measurement. Following are some questions to support learners in all content areas:

- What do you think your designed solution will change? (*hypothesis*)
- What will you observe to determine if your solution works? What will you measure, and how will you measure it? Is it a changed behavior, a change in plant growth, an improved understanding of linear equations? (*variables*)
- What is the one thing you'll measure in testing your designed solution or prototype? (*dependent variables*)

- What factors will remain constant in your designed solution or prototype? (*independent variables*)
- How do you know you're measuring what you need to measure? (*validity*)
- How many times or with how many different individuals should you test your designed solution to ensure it is or isn't consistently successful? (*reliability*)

Using Logic Models to Assess Your Prototype

Visual representations of what we hope our prototypes accomplish are a helpful way of measuring their success and identifying areas for improvement. Researchers use tools such as logic models to develop and measure meaningful change as they scale solutions (Blase, Fixsen, & Jackson, 2015). You can easily apply these tools to the designed solutions created in the classroom.

Building off root-cause analysis, logic models require a concrete representation of anticipated outcomes before testing the prototype. This guides the *test* element and ensures that what is measured is important (i.e., valid). The two overarching components of this phase include planned work (resources and activities) and intended results (outputs, outcomes, and impact).

A revised logic model for design thinking classrooms may include categories such as knowledge and resources, research and actions, designed solution, anticipated outcomes, and impact over time (see Figure 7.3). In this model, students are primed to recall the work they've conducted, alongside the concrete evidence they'll collect to support or reject their designed solution.

A logic model serves as a visual road map for students as they test their prototype, clarifying student assumptions of understanding and anticipated outcomes. With a clear model, students move into the element of *test* and immediately see the efficacy of their designed solution or prototype. Figure 7.4 is an example of what a filled-out logic model might look like for an idea to use a play as a way to improve environmental consciousness.

FIGURE 7.3

A Logic Model for Design Thinking Classrooms

Knowledge and Resources	Research and Actions	Designed Solution	Anticipated Outcomes	Impact over Time
Knowledge: What is the overarching question? How does your content knowledge address the question? **Resources:** What additional resources did you seek?	**Research:** Where did you look to discover the root cause of this problem? **Actions:** What evidence did you use to ensure you had identified the root cause?	**Designed solution:** What did you build, design, create, plan, or enact to solve for your overarching question or problem? What will the designed solution do? Will the solution change behavior, learning, feelings, other?	**Anticipated outcome:** How will you know if your solution worked? What are **each** of the specific indicators you will look for?	**Impact over time:** If your solution is successful, how will it impact a person or system? How will that impact change over time?

FIGURE 7.4

Sample Completed Logic Model: Promoting Environmental Consciousness

Knowledge and Resources	Research and Actions	Designed Solution	Anticipated Outcomes	Impact over Time
Knowledge: Trees provide shade, shelter, and air. One tree provides oxygen for four people. New developments in the neighborhood are cutting down trees. **Resources:** We collected air sample data and compared them to previous years' data and saw that the problem has gotten worse over time.	**Research:** What other natural resources provide shade, shelter, and air? Who is responsible for new construction? What actions can our families take to counter negative effects of tree removal? **Actions:** Research resources, actions, and possible solutions.	**Designed solution:** Create a play that explains the way trees improve our neighborhood and invite parents, teachers, and the entire community.	**Anticipated outcome:** Ask community members to fill out a five-question survey before the play and the same survey after to see if they learned about our resources. Then ask community members to pledge to do one thing that improves the environment each week.	**Impact over time:** Follow up with community members over the next month, in six months, and at the end of the one year to see if they have kept their pact to be environmentally conscious and see if they can still recall how resources are important over time.

Student and Teacher Questions During Test

During the element of *test*, the depth and breadth of the test rest largely on the overarching question, "What outcomes will I look for to determine whether or not my prototype is a solution to the identified issue?" Answering this question requires students to collect data to provide feedback about the efficacy of their solution.

Whether the student is revising his or her daily schedule, creating a play, or collecting groundwater, testing solutions vary based on the question asked and the anticipated answer. For the student seeking to address stressful mornings and routine tardiness, the purpose of the testing was to determine whether an earlier wake-up time would result in an on-time arrival at school. He decided to collect multiple data points each day: when he went to bed at night, when he woke up in the morning, and what time he arrived at school. The teacher asked him to try this method for a week and report on his findings.

To support students in testing their designed solutions, overarching questions help clarify anticipated outcomes. Both teacher and student questions center on the way students identify and test variables. However, **teacher** questions focus largely on supporting learners. For example, are students

- Clearly identifying a single outcome or dependent variable?
- Holding all other variables constant in their test?
- Collecting information about the identified concern?
- Collecting enough information to inform their decision about the effectiveness of their design?
- Communicating their findings clearly and making inferences from their data?
- Testing a prototype that is aligned to the intended curriculum?
- Demonstrating additional content knowledge beyond the standards-aligned content, including skills in communication, critical thinking, and creative problem solving?

In contrast, **student** questions serve as opportunities to connect with peers and demonstrate mastery. They might include any of the following:

- What do I think my designed solution will change? (*dependent variables*)
- What other factors are part of testing my designed solution? (*independent variables*)
- How will I determine if my design solution made an impact? What questions will I ask? What behaviors can I observe?
- How long should I test this solution to know if it's successful?
- How does testing this designed solution help me better understand the content we're discussing in class?
- What knowledge or skills am I gaining by testing the designed solution?

Formative Assessment During *Test*

In addition to modeling the application of standards-based content knowledge, the process of testing demonstrates a host of important skills. By setting his alarm to arrive earlier each day, the perpetually tardy student demonstrated self-regulation skills. By determining the type and length of the test, he showed good critical-thinking skills. Finally, his work was an authentic application of scientific inquiry.

In this way, the element of *test* provides high-quality formative feedback to educators that

- Evaluates how well students used content knowledge and research to develop a solution.
- Determines how students designed solutions to meet the needs of the person or system.
- Identifies how students used feedback from testing their prototype.
- Ascertains the connections students make between feedback from testing and their defined problem.
- Demonstrates how students apply scientific methods to measure the outcome of their designed solution.

Student Self-Assessment During *Test*

Students may be more critical or more lenient of their work than their peers or teachers (Brown, Andrade, & Chen, 2015). That's why self-assessment is more productive when students use it to reflect on their *process* rather than on their product. Self-assessments during the element of *test* should focus on identifying methods that proved successful and those that might need support so students can home in on specific ways to change their approach in the future (Sadler & Good, 2006).

Student self-assessments during the element of *test* reinforce successful problem-solving strategies and support the ongoing development of meta-cognitive skills (see Figure 7.5). This bolsters student beliefs about how knowledge is formed (epistemology) and places students in the active role of knowledge constructor instead of simply receiver. Asking focused questions guides students to reflect critically and objectively on their work and creates valuable opportunities for reflective dialogue with peers and educators.

Peer Assessment During *Test*

Peer feedback is essential during the element of *prototype and test* because it often comes from a more relatable place to students—their peers. Again, the sandwich method helps students identify two particularly interesting or impressive aspects and one area where the peer can ask a clarifying question or provide a clear suggestion that might improve the design or test (see Figure 7.6).

For instance, what questions do other students have about the way a student collected data on their designed solution? How might the student have collected those data differently? How might peers look at the results from the collected data differently than the reviewee? The focus is on how students can support one another's thinking; they're also identifying potential skills and methods to apply in their own work moving forward.

Remember our tardy student? He reflected on the collected data and his process. A full week's worth of data demonstrated that changing *only* his wake-up time had no impact on his arrival at school. He had included three measures of time: bedtime, wake-up, and arrival at school. Were there missing data? After self- and peer review, the student decided to expand his data collection by collecting data on wake-up times and breakfast times for each person in his house.

FIGURE 7.5

Student Self-Assessment Questions During *Test*

Type of Knowledge	Questions for Student Self-Assessment
Metacognition: Knowing About Knowing	• How did you know which measures to use to collect feedback? • How did you know the measures you used were related to your design solution? • What feedback changed the way you thought about your design solution? • Are there any measures you'd like to add now that this test is over?
Self-Regulated Learning: Skills for Learning	• What measures did you use to collect feedback on your designed solution? • How well did the user or system testing your design solution match the intended user? • Are there changes you would make to the process of collecting feedback next time? • What method during *test* would you like help strengthening? What method during *test* do you feel confident about using? • What would you do differently if you could redo the element of *test?*
Epistemological Beliefs: Beliefs About Knowledge	• How do you think experts in _____ area grow their knowledge about _____? • What do you know about the current designed solution for your problem? Who created it? How did they design the solution?
Social-Emotional Learning	• How did you feel during the element of *test?* • How did you communicate with your peers during the element of *test?* • What is a place where you can add your strengths to improve the process of a peer? Where is a place where you would like to seek out support of your peer to improve your areas needing strength?

FIGURE 7.6

Peer Assessment During *Test*

To create feedback for growth, students share two *different* areas of strength surrounding one area for growth.

Feedback for Growth = + +

Area of Strength	**Area for Growth**
Collaborating with you helped me see _____ better because you _____.	I wonder what would have happened if you had measured _____ during the test?
When you decided to do ___ during testing, you inspired me to try _____ because _____.	Do you think _____ would have happened if you had tried _____ to solve for _____?
The way you looked at _____ during the test was interesting because _____.	Something I learned during testing was _____, which may help you _____ differently?
The way you solved _____ helped me better solve/understand _____.	The way you tested for _____ was interesting because it made me think about other ways to do _____.

A week later, the student noticed a pattern in his new data: Although *his* earlier wake-up time didn't change his arrival time, on days when his *parent* woke up earlier, he was no longer late. Taking one more week to test this hypothesis, the student had an answer: When his parent woke up just seven minutes earlier, there was less stress each morning and the student was able to get to school on time.

– Notes from the Field –

Teacher educator Matt Farber worked with 6th and 7th grade social studies students at Valleyview Middle School in Denville, New Jersey, before earning his doctorate and taking his passion for technology, innovation, and pedagogy into higher education. His approach to teaching is founded on the autonomy, competence, and relatedness essential for motivation and learning, and his defining mode for engaging learners is games.

Like many educators who use games for learning, Farber knows that we learn best through play. Games are a low-stakes way to learn, make mistakes, and not be afraid to try all over again. Moreover, through decades of research, Farber and others have found that when kids are engaged in learning through games, they're not only engaging in applying deep content knowledge, they're also honing the important skills of communicating, solving problems, and taking perspective (Boltz, 2019; Diamond, 2012; Farber & Schrier, 2017; Schrier, 2017).

Using commercially available games as a starting point, Farber invited his students to prototype their own games for learning. The point? To help students develop historical empathy—that is, the ability to take the perspective of characters throughout history. Farber selected the game One Night Ultimate Werewolf; at 10 minutes per round, Werewolf is a fast-paced game that accommodates up to eight players at a time. It also includes multiple roles for students to take on while trying to discover which player is the werewolf. After students played the game, Farber unpacked their experience through an empathy conversation, tying the students' game experience to the Salem witch trials. Students then launched into reading content from traditional and graphic sources, including Arthur Miller's play *The Crucible*. At that point, Farber challenged them to "reskin" the game with characters from their learning by simulating what it would feel like to be called a witch during this time period.

Using the game as their model, students quickly got to work reskinning cards to include characters from their *Crucible* readings, from Reverend Hale and Rebecca Nurse to John Proctor and Reverend Parris. To create their cards, students had to understand why each character behaved as they did. For instance, how might Parris's behavior change based on his desire to maintain his reputation in the community? Their goal was to represent the essence of the characters and give players the opportunity to take the perspective of or empathize with each character. Groups of students worked to create paper prototypes of their game. Students added new cards, adjusting and reworking roles to improve the flow of the game until they were happy with the result. Perhaps the most inspiring outcome wasn't seen until the end of the year. Once the books were packed away and many classes were watching movies about the content they'd learned, all that Farber's students wanted to do was take out their reskinned One Night Ultimate Werewolf games to play over and over again.

8

...

Iterate and Reflect:
Reinforcing the Power of Formative Feedback

*We delight in the beauty of the butterfly, but rarely
admit the changes it has gone through to achieve that beauty.*

Maya Angelou

Sachem Central School District is one of the largest school districts on Long Island, New York, with its 12 elementary schools, two junior high schools, one school for 9th and 10th graders, and another one for 11th and 12th graders. So when community members voted to institute a new full-day kindergarten program throughout the district, it was clear that the 16 buildings would have to be completely redesigned to meet the needs of an influx of young students. The district wanted to be sure that incoming kindergartners would love coming to school. They also knew that the old, tired buildings wouldn't create an optimal learning environment for young learners who were in a full day of class for perhaps the first time in their lives.

What's more, the district wanted to rethink the way the buildings were used to increase a sense of community and foster pride in students about their learning environment. With graduating classes of over a thousand students, few had the opportunity to join a school team, act in a school play, or even be seen as an individual. The question was how to build a better kindergarten while also redesigning school buildings and shifting the culture so all students would feel as though they belonged to a unique learning community.

The district hired a design firm that began by asking questions. They asked the youngest learners, "What do you remember about being in kindergarten?" Children were quick to share how the spaces were so much bigger than they were, that the furniture was difficult to use, and that it was hard to play Simon Says because the tables were in the way. More questions followed: Which furniture, colors, and patterns would excite the kindergartners? How should the space be structured to make room for inquiry and discovery while meeting the shifting needs in education? A three-phase process was decided on, with four buildings being redesigned at a time. This would allow engineers and school officials to iterate and reflect on the designs at each step before continuing forward.

Listening to teacher and student concerns about the placement of tables in the older classrooms, the architects and engineers decided to go with adjustable furniture during the first phase of design; they realized that when there were fewer permanent structures inside the classroom, everyone seemed happier. Permanent storage and other interesting spaces would live along the outside of the room. A single table off to one side of each kindergarten room would feature two functional sinks, one on each side, with work space in between for guided reading or center activities. Along the side of the single fixed structure were bookshelves, cubbies for storage, and areas where children could sit comfortably while sharing a book or an activity.

Progress continued with constant iteration and revision, and at the end of the process, the district was wholly redesigned. The 12 elementary schools now housed full-day kindergartners. Four new middle school buildings served students in grades 6–8, with two distinct high schools each housing students from grade 9 through 12. With more buildings came smaller cohorts of students. Where once there were more than a thousand students in a graduating class, now there were a slightly more personable 500. Fewer students per cohort meant that more students could join clubs or sports teams, and a stronger sense of community followed.

The transformation at Sachem was not without a great deal of iteration and reflection. Although the district and architects did much adjusting on the fly, they observed and then adjusted their plans to create what worked best for students. According to Dave Sammel, principal of Sammel Architecture, the design firm that did the work, "If you layer the solution, you often put in place the infrastructure that's needed and let the whole design evolve to meet the needs of the end user. You can keep what works and fix the stuff that doesn't." And that's the beauty and elegance of designing solutions that encourage, value, and use iteration to improve the experiences of everyone.

Guiding Questions for *Iterate and Reflect*

Iterate and reflect are not unique to design thinking; they're essential elements of successful learning environments. Exit tickets and brief check-in conversations are reflections that happen each day in classrooms. Instilling intentional practices of iteration and reflection provides students with the opportunity to see a growth mindset in action. It also gives educators a front row seat while learners apply, deepen, and stretch their knowledge. This is why we became educators—to watch our students soar, knowing the ladder we've scaffolded will help them reach the stars.

Using the lens of design thinking, the element of *iterate and reflect* is a synthesis of the best of cognitive science. Students are actively called to think about their thinking and either revise their designed solution or identify crucial characteristics of the solution that aided in its success. These practices reinforce metacognitive and self-regulated learning strategies.

During this final element of design thinking, two guiding questions emerge. The guiding question during *iterate* asks, "Do parts of the prototype require revision, or do I need to return to a previous element?" Embedded within the question is careful observation of the designed solution. Whether designing a campaign to end bullying or a safer walkway in front of the school, learners must consider the various attributes of their design and how each may or may not have supported the outcome.

The second question digs deep into the process underlying the designed solutions. The driving question during reflect asks, "What steps did I use in designing my solution, and which parts of that process would I change, revise, or repeat in the future?" Here, students reflect on how they apply content knowledge and how they persist when they're at a dead end, improving their perseverance in the face of failure.

Student and Teacher Questions During *Iterate and Reflect*

The iterative process of design thinking increases student voice as learners reflect on their application of knowledge. Over time, it also increases students' ease in applying crucial problem-solving skills across the curriculum and in their own lives (Panadero, Brown, & Strijbos, 2016). What's more, this iterative process enables teachers to regularly identify the skills their learners possess and the practices they employ, giving teachers the opportunity to continually engage students in skill building

The overarching student and teacher questions during *iterate and reflect* focus on specific skills such as problem solving, critical thinking, divergent thinking, and reframing problems or questions. These questions also focus on the types of noncognitive skills that support successful learners, such as the ability to move forward despite setbacks.

Overarching questions for **students** during *iterate and reflect* include the following:

- How does the designed solution make use of the course content?
- Which aspects of the designed solution were successful?
- Which aspects of the designed solution may require additional iteration or revision?
- What design thinking element would best support the iteration or revision that the designed solution needs?
- How is knowledge evolving and changing, and how can this designed solution and the learning from this work help contribute to what we know about this content?

And here are some overarching questions for **teachers** during *iterate and reflect*:

- Are students connecting feedback from their designed solution to applying their content knowledge?
- Can students provide evidence in support of the successful aspects of their design?
- Can students provide evidence in support of the aspects of their design that may need revision?

- If students identify aspects that need revision, can they identify which element of the design thinking process would best support those revisions?
- Have students revised their beliefs about the nature of knowledge and learning as iterative and constantly changing?

Formative Assessment in *Iterate and Reflect*

There are four main goals of formative feedback during the element of *iterate and reflect*. These goals can be used to guide reflective practices throughout the school year as students learn to apply feedback to move forward in their learning. The goals of formative feedback at this stage in the process include the ability to

- Observe how students connect feedback to initial content knowledge and anticipated outcomes of the prototype.
- Identify which aspects of feedback students use to revise their design.
- Assess how students use feedback to revise designs.
- Support students in seeing the iterative process of learning.

Student Self-Assessment During *Iterate and Reflect*

Student use of self-assessments during the element of *iterate and reflect* reinforces successful problem-solving strategies by asking learners to consider the feedback they've received and how that feedback may be used to improve their designed solution or prototype. For instance, the consistently tardy student in our previous chapter looked at the data collected after a week of earlier wake-up times and saw that he was still arriving late to school.

Graphic organizers are a useful mode of making learning visible as students conduct self-assessment during this element (Fisher, Frey, & Hattie, 2016). An effective tool to use here is reminiscent of a KWL chart, with some significant revisions. Traditional KWL charts include three columns aligned to what students know, want to know, and have learned during the process. The three columns in the revised graphic organizer, the

Application-Process-Future Model, ask students to reflect on the *application* of their knowledge, the *process* underlying this application, and how they can use these skills and this knowledge moving forward in the *future* (see Figure 8.1). As they look at their process for thinking and learning, students deepen their ability to use self-regulation in their learning and learn to think about their thinking.

Using the Application-Process-Future Model for self-assessment shifts the focus toward active learning and helps support a can-do attitude. Students are able to see how each action moves through a natural progression while allowing for revisions and improvements in the future, reinforcing the iterative nature of knowledge acquisition and reframing students as change makers and knowledge builders.

With this tool, the application of knowledge to real-world problem solving is readily apparent to each member of the community, from teachers and students to parents and administrators. Imagine a gallery walk where this type of graphic organizer of student thought is paired with a narrative or prototype of the designed solution. Inviting students to curate their experience in this way fosters autonomy, reinforces competence, and illustrates that each learner is an integral part of the classroom community.

Peer Assessment During *Iterate and Reflect*

Peer feedback provided during this element should be specific and positive, offering opportunities for growth and reflecting on the ways in which each student approached their solution differently. This feedback can provide valuable insight into individual differences in communication and approaches to problem solving.

When students offer feedback *to peers with whom they've collaborated* on a solution, they can reflect on the following prompts:

- Explain something your peer did that was helpful or encouraging during the elements of design thinking.
- Describe a time when your peer did something inspiring and why it was inspiring.

FIGURE 8.1

Application-Process-Future Model

Application	Process	Future
The solution I designed was meant to solve _____.	One way I did this was to _____.	In the future, I might try _____ because it may help _____.
This solution required the application of _____ content from our course.	The content was helpful in understanding _____.	I wonder how I can apply _____ to designing a solution in the future.
This solution required me to seek out _____ (describe information, resources, and feedback needed).	I was able to find this information _____.	Moving forward, I'd like to try looking to _____ sources for additional information, support, or feedback.
I believe the _____ feedback I received from _____ would help make changes to my designed solution because _____.	To apply this feedback, I'd need to _____.	In the future, I'd ask for specific feedback about _____ to help me better _____.
The _____ feedback might change _____ to my designed solution.	I could measure the success of _____ change by doing _____.	One way I'd try a new approach to measuring a solution in the future would be to _____.
I can test this feedback in subsequent testing by looking for changes to _____.	One way I can prepare to do this will be _____.	The element that would support this change would be the element of _____ (understand and empathize, identify and research, communicate to ideate, prototype and test, or iterate and reflect).
The _____ feedback helped me support/reject) my designed solution because _____.	A way I can use this feedback to see if it is helpful is to _____.	One element of design thinking I'd like to review to see if this feedback is helpful is the element of _____.
The _____ feedback was/was not aligned to my anticipated outcome of _____ because _____.	I can tell that this feedback is/is not aligned to my outcome by _____.	Moving forward, an area or element of design thinking in which I'd like to receive different or more feedback is _____ because _____.

- Share something great you learned from your peer, such as communicating clearly, being patient, explaining content, thinking of new ways to express ideas, and so on.
- Present an area in which you'd like to work with your peer again and describe what you'd like to get out of a future collaboration.

When giving peer feedback *on other students' designed solutions*, the reviewing student should look over the peer's completed Application-Process-Future organizer because it encourages students to provide feedback about the *process* their peers used to solve complex problems. After looking through the organizer, students might consider the following questions as they formulate their feedback:

- What is one way your peer applied content to solve a problem that was particularly impressive?
- What process did your peer use that you'd like to learn more about and try?
- What is one way your peer used feedback to change the designed solution?
- What idea might you suggest that could help your peer think differently about the designed solution?
- How might you collaborate with your peer in the future to design a solution?

Inviting students to conduct peer assessment has demonstrated a positive impact on learning (Li, Liu, & Steckelberg, 2010) and may also increase a student's ability to take perspective. What's more, the reflective lens of a peer in addition to that of self-provided and teacher-provided feedback reinforces important processes for learning and solidifies understanding.

Design Thinking Redux

During the element of *iterate and reflect*, student self- and peer assessments provide rich feedback that ensures students can identify whether their solution requires additional changes (iteration) or whether they're satisfied with their results. If an iteration is necessary, learners need to revisit one of the elements of design thinking that may improve their solution.

But how can students identify which element to revisit? The flowchart in Figure 8.2 helps guide learners through the various elements of design thinking and can pinpoint where a problem might reside.

More Than the Sum of Its Parts

At a large public Title 1 school in New York City, morning meetings typically ended with kindergartners choosing which center they would visit that day. By mid-December, some of the novelty of the centers had worn off. The children were still smitten with the dress-up area with its community helper theme, and they were still frequent visitors to the interview station where they would each get a clipboard and move from center to center asking students about, for example, their preference for Ninjago or Wonder Pets. But by December, the block center was the odd one out.

One morning, Dana Roth turned to her students and said, "This block center isn't keeping us as energized as the other centers. What can we do about it?" The flurry of suggestions that followed included replacing the blocks with dinosaurs, building a bigger kitchen area—and adding a water park. Seeing an opportunity to raise student voice and choice, the teacher challenged her students: "Let's see if some of us using the block center today can find a job to help this center become more useful."

The first day of the challenge found students discussing their upcoming holiday plans. One child talked about taking a plane to visit family. Several children had never visited an airport, much less taken a flight before, so they used the blocks to create what they imagined an airport might look like. It was an organic process, and the children discussed which blocks would work best for a runway or make a better structure where "people wait for their plane to leave." The rectangular ones or the triangular ones? How tall should the building be where the people sit and wait for the planes? And how long should a runway be for a plane to be able to take off?

As the class period drew to a close, the children were deflated thinking they had to take apart their beautiful structure. That's when inspiration

FIGURE 8.2

Design Thinking Flowchart

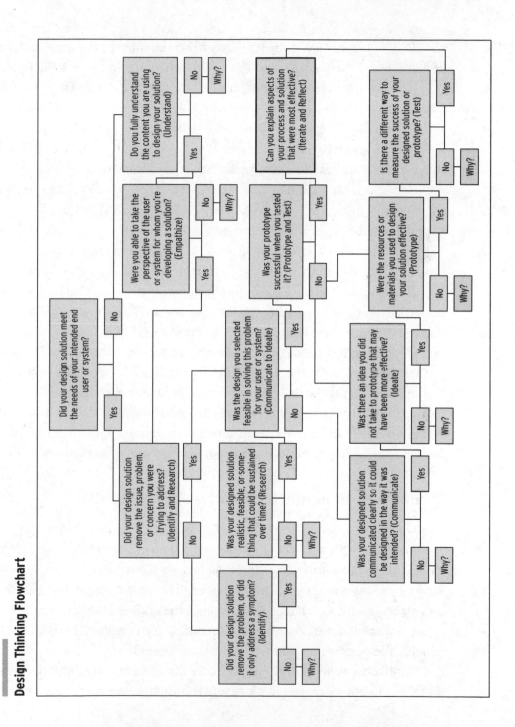

struck. The teacher asked the children from the interview station to take a poll and see if the class wanted to put the center to work—as an active airport. Interviewers tallied student choices, and it was settled: The center had a new job.

Grabbing a roll of masking tape, Dana asked students to put tape on the parts of the structure that should stay in place and not be returned to the box that day. Over time, all students would have the chance to add to this collaborative creation. The next day, the teacher reached out to a local heliport, and the students helped her compose a letter of inquiry: "Might our class visit your heliport to do research for our new block center?"

What started as a simple inquiry to gauge student interest in a tool turned into a full unit of study on aviation. The students used skills in art, math, science, history, and literacy as they unofficially engaged in different elements of design thinking. After visiting the heliport and interviewing pilots, students iterated on their designs and ultimately transformed their airport into a heliport. During reflection, they wrote thank-you letters to those who had aided in their learning, from the pilot to the docent at the hanger. The notes were a summative assessment demonstrating the rich knowledge they'd gained. Perhaps most important, the students began to wonder, "What if we could rethink the way we use our math bins to create new games?" The process invited wonder into the classroom and deepened the joy of learning.

Design Solutions and Summative Assessment

The word *summation* is derived from the Latin *summatus*, or adding up. The "adding up" of the skills acquired and honed during each element of design thinking may be greater than the designed solution, as the example of the kindergartners and their heliport showed. This approach is student driven and places learners in charge of seeking out the knowledge they need.

But what about summative assessment? The elements of design thinking provide the opportunity to summatively assess students in four areas: application of content knowledge, use of soft skills, personal learning outcomes, and shifts in approaches to thinking and learning.

Application of content knowledge. Traditional models of curriculum and instruction present content, provide opportunity to practice, assess learning with a test, and move along. The elements of design thinking flip traditional models by reframing "opportunity to practice" as "opportunity to apply." This approach might appear to make learning more complex, but what it actually does is make learning more meaningful.

For example, instead of simply distinguishing between cubism and impressionism in an art class, students in design thinking classrooms must consider the context behind each artistic movement—the affordances of the media, the contexts of each artist, the cultural concepts that influenced their work, the impact their work had on the world around them—as students work to create designs that best represent these same aspects in their own lives. Or instead of filling out a worksheet by selecting the correct spelling word to complete a sentence, students might use the words in novel and meaningful ways by putting on a play to increase community awareness of pollution or creating a commercial for why their school should implement a different schedule.

Use of soft skills. Foundational content skills are hallmarks of traditional education, and for good reason. However, the most essential skills for future-ready learners are those that require the uniquely human capabilities of synthesis and collaboration, productive deliberation, and consensus building. Successful learners are those who can effectively ask questions, seek solutions, conduct research, share and present ideas, and receive and provide feedback from peers and teachers. In the design thinking classroom, students are called on to consider their process for learning, observe and learn from their peers, and see firsthand that they have agency and voice as learners.

Personal learning outcomes. As learners become accustomed to this scaffolded approach to knowledge discovery and application, their attributions for learning may change. Taking on ownership of problem solving supports students in developing a sense of autonomy and voice. Inviting them to revisit concepts as they design, create, and enact their solutions makes the language of growth mindset concrete. What's more, when students practice regular revisions to their work with the support and feedback of peers and educators, they learn that their process and progress are more important than the product.

Shifts in approaches to thinking and learning. The elements of design thinking reinforce the powerful shifts that occur when learning is presented as co-constructed or, better yet, still evolving. Students come to see that their curiosity has value, their questions are worthwhile, their abilities are always growing, and their contributions will change the world. The element of *iterate and reflect* invites each student to take a bird's-eye view of their work to see clearly how far their learning has grown.

– Notes from the Field –

Barbara Gruener's career spans content, curriculum, and contexts, as she worked with students in English, Spanish, and English as a second language classrooms before taking on the role of counselor and character coach. Over her three-plus decades in education, she has collaborated with thousands of students and educators to amass an impressive catalogue of resources in support of the element *iterate and reflect*, including a multimodal experience called the Peace Labyrinth (see Figure 8.3).

Created by Jay Stailey and Reginald Adams, the Peace Labyrinth is a physical learning experience requiring two learners to enter with disparate thoughts, goals, or opinions. While responding to a series of prompts, they move through the labyrinth, and by the time they meet to exit together, they're far more connected than when they began.

Gruener uses the labyrinth to facilitate successful conflict resolution in what she calls the Pathway to Peace. She adapted a five-question framework from her Minnesota school, aligning each prompt to a specific position in the labyrinth. Students had to (1) state the problem; (2) state their feelings; (3) state the other person's feelings; (4) brainstorm solutions; and (5) choose the best solution before exiting together. The simple problem Gruener models is based on two conflicting choices of where to go for lunch. Students choose their favorite places, and two students are selected that have competing selections. As they move through the labyrinth, students practice listening to understand instead of listening to reply. When you're focused on defending why your restaurant *does* have better fries, you fail to listen to your peer who wants to go to her restaurant, which has great fries, is where her sister works, and may provide a special treat to visiting friends and family. This shift in truly listening to others is the bridge to taking the perspective of another.

"It's important to note that step three is where students develop empathy; it's also the place where students are the most distant physically," Gruener

FIGURE 8.3

Peace Labyrinth Model

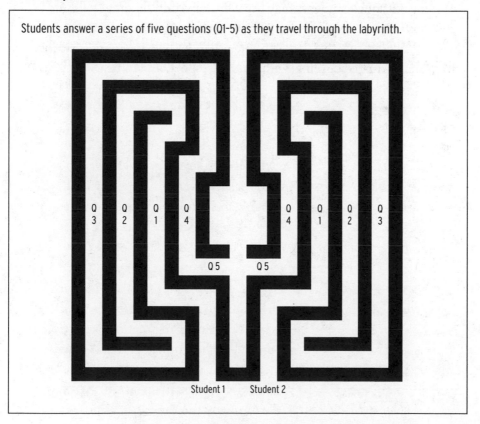

explained. "Step three requires students to step outside themselves to take the perspective of their peer." If the student wasn't listening to what the other person had to say, they're unable to move forward, and it's a stalemate. The process of moving through the path to peace helps students really listen to their peers and reflect on the feelings of an "other."

The labyrinth invites discourse about where to iterate on a design or practice taking perspective in an active and applied way. And although the labyrinth at Gruener's school was painted on the concrete outside the school building, other schools have used tarps or painter's tape on the classroom floor to ensure the labyrinth can be transported or used indoors.

Individual students may begin worlds apart, and through the shared experience, their perspectives ebb and flow alongside their developing understanding. Although students may leave the labyrinth holding the same beliefs they entered into it with, their ability to communicate and listen has enabled them to take perspective, develop empathy for their peer, and exit together with a shared understanding, with mutual respect, and in peace.

9

...

Applying Knowledge to Practice:
Isn't That the Point?

The most common way people give up their power
is by thinking they don't have any.

Alice Walker

Fauquier High School is a large public school in Warrenton, Virginia. With its multiple buildings, it feels more like a college campus than a high school. The layout made it complicated for colleagues to meet with one another regularly; many felt a sense of disconnection and isolation. Not looking to do a complete redesign of the campus, the school nevertheless wanted to find a common space where students and staff could build community. One educator drew inspiration from the school's front lobby and hallways.

George Murphy, a science educator at Fauquier, realized that although he couldn't change the structure of the buildings, he *could* design a space to build community. School faculty and students gather each morning and evening in the main lobby of the school; with its bare white walls, it was literally a blank template. Murphy's idea was to create an interdisciplinary mural. It would be a living timeline, a visual representation documenting the tremendous amount of knowledge acquired within the walls of the school. The mural would begin in the lobby and wind its way throughout the halls. It would invite conversation and foster connections.

Each department was asked to contribute to the living timeline. Murphy's advanced placement biology students started in the lobby, representing their learning through rich visual imagery across chronological and physical space.

Soon other departments began adding to the timeline, where scientifically accurate models of the ocean's layers are depicted alongside images of historical figures and technologies that drove these innovations. Learners were able to see the connections among such disparate fields as medicine, technology, and history. They saw how technological innovations like X-ray diffraction set the stage for medical discoveries like DNA, leading the way for a deeper understanding of genetics and disease.

What began as a problem of connection and community turned into a celebration of learning and growth. Murphy set out to bring faculty, staff, and students together to make visible the great work happening across the school buildings. In the process, he showed learners how knowledge itself is not siloed and depends on collaboration. The timeline is subtle, living along the bottom of the school walls, but because it's continually updated, it will grow to represent the voices of the many learners who fill the school halls. What's more, Murphy has integrated the timeline with his lessons to include scavenger hunts that explore the timeline across multiple domains. Other educators are following suit, and learners, too, are finding ways to celebrate this community knowledge installation, proudly showing siblings and parents their contribution to this interdisciplinary demonstration of knowledge.

Humanness—The Key to the Future

Across school districts and grade levels, educators and learners are working diligently to reframe the way that school is done by embracing innovative methods of teaching and learning, such as design thinking. What has become clear is that the success of each individual won't come from besting a computer but rather by using our innately human capacities of talking with others to debate, discuss, and develop dynamic solutions toward our shared goals. Murphy's interdisciplinary timeline solved the problem of a seemingly disconnected school community, but it also solved a much larger issue in our school system: The subjects we teach, from physics to math to literature, exist as isolated topics. With his timeline, Murphy presented knowledge as it truly is, interconnected and evolving.

We all agree that school should change, but we often get stuck in the *how*. Design thinking is not a single answer but one of a suite of solutions that can pave the way to more meaningful learning. The elements within design thinking are an open invitation for those who wish to prepare our learners to take on roles in this complex landscape that is our current and future reality.

Design thinking is often cited as human-centered design, but it's really a method of applying knowledge to practice. Isn't this also the definition of teaching? The applied nature of knowledge inherent in elements of design thinking moves beyond the worksheets of the past to support learners in being the critical thinkers, problem solvers, and creators of a better tomorrow.

The Elements of Incremental Change

Together we've examined research-based support for enacting the lens of design thinking in classrooms to create meaningful learning alongside the shifting roles of educators and learners. We then unpacked the five elements of design thinking: understand and empathize, identify and research, communicate to ideate, prototype and test, and iterate and reflect. Finally, we looked at many fine examples of how educators are using design thinking to create extraordinary learning experiences. Readers saw

- How a permission slip gave permission to educators to innovate in their classrooms.
- How strategies such as a "snowball" fight and "me soup" enabled teachers and students to learn more about one another.
- How a robot wedding set the stage for students to learn complex coding skills.
- How a podcast project involved students in researching the impact of important events on peoples' lives.
- How a communications blitz addressed the root cause of concerns about standards-based grading.
- How a "thought partnership" between two teachers resulted in students taking turns teaching their peers.

- How game play became a compelling approach to teaching history.
- How a student-created mail system addressed a classroom's sense of isolation from the rest of the school.
- How students used a block center to jump-start a unit on aviation.
- How a teaching strategy facilitated mutual respect and promoted peace.

Technology will continue to accelerate at breakneck speed, creating new solutions to both old and new problems. But our students will still need to possess foundational skills to be able to see what's underneath the hood when things break in our technology-enhanced world. The elements of design thinking and ongoing formative feedback support learners as they navigate learning, take ownership, and proudly become the problem solvers of tomorrow.

Teaching and Learning What You Love

So what's the secret sauce behind the educators enacting such significant changes within the four walls of their classroom? Associate teaching professor Chris Unger, in the Graduate School of Education at Boston's Northeastern University, has some ideas: "School is the way it is because we don't engage in design thinking to design schools." Several years back, Unger was invited to have a conversation with a small group of educators at Lyndon Institute, a private high school in Vermont. Because the town lacked a public high school, all students in the district were able to go to the private school through public school funding.

Ten educators from the school were invited to the conversation. After they briefly introduced themselves, Unger politely interjected, "But you're not telling me about *you*. Who are you? And what do you love to do?" After a moment of silence, the educators began to share: Some loved rock climbing; another was a local disc jockey. These educators had worked together for years and were only now realizing their shared passions.

And then it was Unger's turn. He told of how he connects educators and innovators across the United States through a shared goal of creating a better system of education. He recounted a story of a little school in Portland,

Oregon, that for an entire week in the middle of each school year allows educators to teach whatever they want to teach and students to sign up for whatever they're most passionate about learning. If you're teaching rock climbing, you won't be sitting in a classroom using a textbook or writing five-paragraph essays. You'll get outside and do some climbing! By merely changing the curriculum to what teachers loved to do, learning changed to *doing*. It became action based, interest based, competency based, and far more engaging for both students and educators.

A few months later, the assistant head of school for curriculum and instruction called Unger to report, "Guess what? We're doing it. But not for just one week—for three!" The program at Lyndon Institute came to be called *J-term*, where each January, students can select one or more courses, such as "She Persists," which explores the lives of women challenging the status quo; "Understanding Happiness"; or what the required skills and wills are for young women to master the gas metal arc welding process in "Women Welders." The program has been running for five years at the school, and both the students and faculty now wonder, "Why can't *this* be school?"

The Hidden Track

So how can a single teacher in a single classroom enact such a tremendous change? It's simple, really—it starts with you. The *real* secret sauce in each classroom across our nation and our globe is the person holding this book right now.

Growing up in an age of cassette tapes, I found that the hidden tracks were the most exciting, those secret tracks shared by the artist that would reveal themselves only to the truly dedicated fans and that were so often missed by the casual listener. Our latent passions and talents are the hidden tracks on a cassette waiting to be revealed and shared with the world. It's the passion within the heart of each educator who wakes up every morning with the goal of supporting learners as they learn and grow that can jump-start this new revolution of learning.

The elements of design thinking can unleash our hidden tracks, and those of our students, to reveal the beautiful diversity each of us brings to the classroom and the many ways we can apply our knowledge to solve pressing problems. Margaret Mead cautioned us that we should "never doubt that a small group of thoughtful, committed citizens can change the world. Indeed, it is the only thing that ever has."

I believe that teachers are that small group of thoughtful and committed citizens engaged in the hard but important work of transforming the nature of learning for the youngest and most important citizens on our planet, our children. You're appreciated, you're valued, and you're making an impact on the world in ways you may never fully know—and for that, I thank you.

Acknowledgments

It was much easier to be a parent before I had children, just as it was much easier to write a book before one was waiting to be written. Thankfully, I'm standing on the shoulders of many remarkable folks whose guidance and support paved my way and for whom I am truly grateful.

I would like to express my deepest gratitude to my fellow educators who so generously shared their stories within these pages. What an honor it is to have to elevate your great work: Amber Coleman-Mortley, Heidi Bernasconi, MaryRose Joseph, Karen Schrier, Jody Drezner Alperin, Vicky Finney Crouch, Vicky Lang, Barbara Bray, Matt Farber, Jay Billy, Laura Steinbrink, Dana Roth, Sarah Fiess, Andrea Henkel, Barbara Gruener, Paula Dillon, Catherine Croft, Adam Norwood, and Emily O'Rourke.

I would also like to thank my two cofounders, Jessica Ochoa Hendrix and Mandë Holford, whose passion for creating immersive learning experiences to bring science out of the lab and into the hands of learners inspires me daily.

It is true that an educator affects eternity, and it was my 6th grade teacher Karl Klimek who showed us we were never too young to dream big and my high school mentors Kristie Paull Syron, Jeannee Turner, and Greg Cleveland who taught us that iteration is never truly over, even after the last curtain falls. I am so very grateful for my mentor Mitchell Rabinowitz, who challenged me to think deeply about the heuristics of problem solving across domains and pushed me to relentlessly question everything (except pinot).

Thank you to the dream team at ASCD, from my brilliant editors Susan Hills and Liz Wegner, whose constructive feedback significantly improved the writing in these pages; to Georgia Park, whose artwork perfectly encapsulates the flexible yet intentional nature of design thinking; to Alexa Epitropoulos, who has impeccable timing and a heart of gold.

A tremendous thank you to my dear friend and colleague Amy Rodriguez, original member of my thought tribe who was and is always willing to provide sincere feedback. A heartfelt thank you to my colleague Chris Unger, a veritable change agent in education and constant source of inspiration whose connections to extraordinary educators globally inspired many of the vignettes in this work. And thank you to Cameron McClure and Jonathan Lyons, whose expertise in writing and friendship has no limits.

Parenting is not for the faint of heart, and I am grateful to my parents who worked endlessly to make sure we had what we needed to thrive.

Thank you to my incredible husband Gary for not only providing regular feedback on each chapter but also wrangling the kids so I could spend another weekend in the stacks of our local library. Thank you for giving me the space and support I needed to bring this passion project to life. For the hugs, love, and affirmations on the days I need it most, I am forever grateful to my two boys, Judah and Levi.

Lastly, I'd like to give thanks to my students, whose feedback pushes me to always be better, and without whom I wouldn't be the one thing that makes me happiest, a teacher.

References

Bambino, D. (2002). Critical friends. *Educational Leadership*, 59(6), 25–27.

Bernacki, M. L., Nokes-Malach, T. J., & Aleven, V. (2015). Examining self-efficacy during learning: Variability and relations to behavior, performance, and learning. *Metacognition and Learning, 10*(1), 99–117.

Blase, K., Fixsen, D., & Jackson, K. R. (2015). Creating meaningful change in education: A cascading logic model. *Scaling-Up Brief,* no. 6. Chapel Hill, NC: State Implementation and Scaling-Up of Evidence-Based Practices Center.

Bloom, B. S. (1956). *Taxonomy of educational objectives. Handbook 1: Cognitive domain*. New York: Longman.

Boltz, L. O. (2019). "Nervousness and maybe even some regret": Videogames and the cognitive-affective model of historical empathy. In Brock R. Dubbels (Ed.), *Exploring the cognitive, social, cultural, and psychological aspects of gaming and simulations* (pp. 228–251). Hershey, PA: IGI Global.

Bray, B. (2015). 10 ways to encourage passion-based learning [Blog post]. Retrieved from https://barbarabray.net/2015/10/11/10-ways-to-encourage-passion-based-learning/

Brown, G. T. L., Andrade, H. L., & Chen, F. (2015). Accuracy in student self-assessment: Directions and cautions for research. *Assessment in Education: Principles, Policy & Practice*, 22(4), 444–457.

Butler, R., & Shibaz, L. (2014). Striving to connect and striving to learn: Influences of relational and mastery goals for teaching on teacher behaviors and student interest and help seeking. *International Journal of Educational Research, 65*, 41–53.

Chambers, T. V. (2009). The "receivement gap": School tracking policies and the fallacy of the "achievement gap." *Journal of Negro Education, 78*(4),417–431.

Chouinard, M. M. (2007). Children's questions: A mechanism for cognitive development: IV. *Monographs of the Society for Research in Child Development, 72*(1), 58–82.

Clark, S., & Seider, S. (2017). Developing critical curiosity in adolescents. *Equity & Excellence in Education, 50*(2), 125–141.

Collins, A., Brown, J. S., & Newman, S. E. (1989). Cognitive apprenticeship: Teaching the crafts of reading, writing, and mathematics. In L. Resnick (Ed.), *Knowing, learning, and instruction: Essays in honor of Robert Glaser* (pp. 453–494). New York: Routledge.

Cook, C. R., Fiat, A., Larson, M., Daikos, C., Slemrod, T., Holland, E. A.,… & Renshaw, T. (2018). Positive greetings at the door: Evaluation of a low-cost, high-yield proactive classroom management strategy. *Journal of Positive Behavior Interventions, 20*(3), 149–159.

Costa, A. L., & Kallick, B. (1993). Through the lens of a critical friend. *Educational Leadership, 51*(2), 49–51.

Craig, S., Graesser, A., Sullins, J., & Gholson, B. (2004). Affect and learning: An exploratory look into the role of affect in learning with AutoTutor. *Journal of Educational Media, 29*(3), 241–250.

Darling-Hammond, L. (2008). Teacher learning that supports student learning. *Teaching for Intelligence, 2*(1), 91–100.

Diamond, J. (2012). "You weren't doing what you would actually do, you were doing what people wanted you to do": A study of historical empathy in a digital history game. Doctoral dissertation, New York University.

Didicher, N. (2016). Bento and buffet: Two approaches to flexible summative assessment. *Collected Essays on Learning and Teaching, 9,* 167–174.

D'Mello, S., Lehman, B., Pekrun, R., & Graesser, A. (2014). Confusion can be beneficial for learning. *Learning and Instruction, 29,* 153–170.

Dweck, C. (2017). *Mindset: Changing the way you think to fulfill your potential* (Rev. ed.). New York: Little, Brown.

Engel, S. (2011). Children's need to know: Curiosity in schools. *Harvard Educational Review, 81*(4), 625–645.

Fahey, K. M. (2011). Still learning about leading: A leadership critical friends group. *Journal of Research on Leadership Education, 6*(1), 1–35.

Fandakova, Y., & Bunge, S. A. (2016). What connections can we draw between research on long-term memory and student learning? *Mind, Brain, and Education, 10*(3), 135–141.

Farber, M., & Schrier, K. (2017). The limits and strengths of using digital games as "empathy machines." Working paper. New Delhi: UNESCO/Mahatma Gandhi Institute for Peace and Sustainable Development (MGIP).

Fisher, D., Frey, N., & Hattie, J. (2016). *Visible learning for literacy, grades K–12: Implementing the practices that work best to accelerate student learning.* Thousand Oaks, CA: Corwin Press.

Freire, P. (2018). *Teachers as cultural workers: Letters to those who dare teach.* New York: Routledge.

Gallagher, A., & Thordarson, K. (2018). *Design thinking for school leaders: Five rules and mindsets that ignite positive change.* Alexandria, VA: ASCD.

Hammond, Z. (2014). *Culturally responsive teaching and the brain: Promoting authentic engagement and rigor among culturally and linguistically diverse students.* Thousand Oaks, CA: Corwin Press.

Hofer, B. K. (2016). Epistemic cognition as a psychological construct: Advancements and challenges. In J. Greene, W. Sandoval, & I. Bråten (Eds.), *Handbook of epistemic cognition* (pp. 19–38). New York: Routledge.

Hulleman, C. S., & Harackiewicz, J. M. (2009). Promoting interest and performance in high school science classes. *Science, 326*(5958), 1410–1412.

Hwang, G. J., Hung, C. M., & Chen, N. S. (2014). Improving learning achievements, motivations, and problem-solving skills through a peer assessment-based game development approach. *Educational Technology Research and Development, 62*(2), 129–145.

Kirschner, P. A. (2017). Stop propagating the learning styles myth. *Computers & Education, 106*, 166–171.

Li, L., Liu, X., & Steckelberg, A. L. (2010). Assessor or assessee: How student learning improves by giving and receiving peer feedback. *British Journal of Educational Technology, 41*(3), 525–536.

Lin-Siegler, X., Dweck, C. S., & Cohen, G. L. (2016). Instructional interventions that motivate classroom learning. *Journal of Educational Psychology, 108*(3), 295.

Manyika, J., Lund, S., Chui, M., Bughin, J., Woetzel, J., Batra, P., . . . & Sanghvi, S. (2017, December). Jobs lost, jobs gained: What the future of work will mean for jobs, skills, and wages. Retrieved from https://www.mckinsey.com/featured-insights/future-of-work/jobs-lost-jobs-gained-what-the-future-of-work-will-mean-for-jobs-skills-and-wages

Markant, D. B., Ruggeri, A., Gureckis, T. M., & Xu, F. (2016). Enhanced memory as a common effect of active learning. *Mind, Brain, and Education, 10*(3), 142–152.

Marsh, E. J., Arnold, K. M., Smith, M. A., & Stromeyer, S. L. (2015). How psychological science can improve our classrooms: Recommendations should bridge the laboratory and the classroom. *Translational Issues in Psychological Science, 1*(2), 127.

Maslow, A. H. (1971). *The farther reaches of human nature.* New York: Arkana/Penguin Books.

Masters, G., & Forster, M. (1996). *Developmental assessment: Assessment resource kit (ARK).* Camberwell, Australia: Australian Council for Educational Research.

Mega, C., Ronconi, L., & De Beni, R. (2014). What makes a good student? How emotions, self-regulated learning, and motivation ontribute to academic achievement. *Journal of Educational Psychology, 106*(1), 121.

Moon, J. A. (2013). *A handbook of reflective and experiential learning: Theory and practice.* New York: Routledge.

Morin, J. (2017). Action Priority Matrix. Retrieved from https://www.linkedin.com/pulse/action-priority-matrix-jason-morin

Morrison, M. (2010). History of SMART objectives. Rapid Business Improvement. Retrieved from https://rapidbi.com/history-of-smart-objectives/

National Research Council. (2003). *Engaging schools: Fostering high school students' motivation to learn.* Washington, DC: National Academies Press.

Oliver, K. M. (2000). Methods for developing constructivism learning on the web. *Educational Technology, 40*(6), 5–18.

Ozturk, T., & Guven, B. (2016). Evaluating students' beliefs in problem-solving process: A case study. *Eurasia Journal of Mathematics, Science & Technology Education, 12*(3), 411–429.

Panadero, E., Brown, G. T., & Strijbos, J. W. (2016). The future of student self-assessment: A review of known unknowns and potential directions. *Educational Psychology Review, 28*(4), 803–830.

Pink, D. H. (2011). *Drive: The surprising truth about what motivates us.* New York: Riverhead Books.

Popham, J. W. (2007). The lowdown on learning progressions. *Educational Leadership, 64*(7), 83–84.

Rands, M. L., & Gansemer-Topf, A. M. (2017). The room itself is active: How classroom design impacts student engagement. *Journal of Learning Spaces, 6*(1), 26.

Richardson, V. (Ed.). (2005). *Constructivist teacher education: Building a world of new understandings.* New York: Routledge.

Riener, C., & Willingham, D. (2010). The myth of learning styles. *Change: The Magazine of Higher Learning, 42*(5), 32–35.

Rohrer, D., & Taylor, K. (2006). The effects of overlearning and distributed practice on the retention of mathematics knowledge. *Applied Cognitive Psychology, 20,* 1209–1244.

Ruzek, E. A., Hafen, C. A., Allen, J. P., Gregory, A., Mikami, A. Y., & Pianta, R. C. (2016). How teacher emotional support motivates students: The mediating roles of perceived peer relatedness, autonomy support, and competence. *Learning and Instruction, 42,* 95–103.

Ryan, R. M., & Deci, E. L. (2000). Self-determination theory and the facilitation of intrinsic motivation, social development, and well-being. *American Psychologist, 55*(1), 68–78.

Sadler, P., & Good, E. (2006). The impact of self- and peer-grading on student learning. *Educational Assessment, 11*(1), 1–31.

Savery, J. R. (2015). Overview of problem-based learning: Definitions and distinctions. In A. Walker, H. Leary, C. Hmelo-Silver, & P. A. Ertmer (Eds.), *Essential readings in problem-based learning: Exploring and extending the legacy of Howard S. Barrows* (pp. 5–15). West Lafayette, IN: Purdue University Press.

Schraw, G., & Gutierrez, A. P. (2015). Metacognitive strategy instruction that highlights the role of monitoring and control processes. In A. Peña-Ayala (Ed.), *Metacognition: Fundaments, applications, and trends* (pp. 3–16). Cham, Switzerland: Springer.

Schrier, K. (2017). Designing games for moral learning and knowledge building. *Games and Culture.* doi:10.1177/1555412017711514.

Schwab, K. (2016). *The fourth industrial revolution.* World Economic Forum. New York: Crown Business.

Sewell, A. (2002). Constructivism and student misconceptions: Why every teacher needs to know about them. *Australian Science Teachers Journal, 48*(4), 24.

Shane-Simpson, C., Che, E., & Brooks, P. J. (2016). Giving psychology away: Implementation of Wikipedia editing in an introductory human development course. *Psychology Learning & Teaching, 15*(3), 268–293.

Smith, C., Wiser, M., Anderson, C. W., & Krajcik, J. (2006). Implications for children's learning for assessment: A proposed learning progression for matter and the atomic molecular theory. *Measurement, 14*(1–2), 1–98.

Sussman, D. (2017). From partisanship to pluralism: Teaching students how to listen to each other. *Phi Delta Kappan, 99*(4), 50–53.

Vygotsky, L. S. (1978). *Mind in society: The development of higher psychological processes* (M. Cole, V. John-Steiner, S. Scribner, & E. Souberman, Trans. & Eds.). Cambridge, MA: Harvard University Press.

Walker, M. A., & Li, Y. (2015). Improving information literacy skills through learning to use and edit Wikipedia: A chemistry perspective. *Journal of Chemical Education, 93*(3), 509–515.

Wiggins, G. P., & McTighe, J. (2011). *The Understanding by Design guide to creating high-quality units*. Alexandria, VA: ASCD.

Winne, P. H. (2017). Cognition and metacognition within self-regulated learning. In D. H. Schunk & J. A. Greene (Eds.), *Handbook of self-regulation of learning and performance* (pp. 52–64). New York: Routledge.

Index

The letter *f* following a page number denotes a figure.

About the Author

**Lindsay Portnoy,** PhD, is a cognitive scientist and consultant working to translate research-based practices in teaching and learning to improve curriculum, assessment, and the intentional integration of emerging practices and tools to support learners. A former public school teacher, Portnoy has spent nearly two decades working in preK–12, higher ed, and informal educational settings. She is an associate teaching professor at Northeastern University's Graduate School of Education and is cofounder and chief learning officer at Killer Snails.

Drawing from a deep knowledge of the process of teaching and learning, Portnoy works with education changemakers from teachers and policymakers to administrators and curriculum developers. Using the best that cognitive science has to offer, she designs, implements, and creates authentic, measurable, and engaging learning experiences to truly level up learning.

Related ASCD Resources

At the time of publication, the following resources were available (ASCD stock numbers in parentheses).

Cultivating Curiosity in K–12 Classrooms: How to Promote and Sustain Deep Learning by Wendy L. Ostroff (#116001)

Design Thinking for School Leaders: Five Roles and Mindsets That Ignite Positive Change by Alyssa Gallagher and Kami Thordarson (#118022)

Learning in the Making: How to Plan, Execute, and Assess Powerful Makerspace Lessons by Jackie Gerstein (#119025)

Project Based Teaching: How to Create Rigorous and Engaging Learning Experiences by Suzie Boss with John Larmer (#118047)

The Relevant Classroom: 6 Steps to Foster Real-World Learning by Eric Hardie (#120003)

Students at the Center: Personalized Learning with Habits of Mind by Bena Kallick and Allison Zmuda (#117015)

Teaching in the Fast Lane: How to Create Active Learning Experiences by Suzy Pepper Rollins (#117024)

What If? Building Students' Problem-Solving Skills Through Complex Challenges by Ronald Beghetto (#118009)

For up-to-date information about ASCD resources, go to **www.ascd.org.** You can search the complete archives of *Educational Leadership* at **www.ascd.org/el.**

ASCD myTeachSource®

Download resources from a professional learning platform with hundreds of research-based best practices and tools for your classroom at http://myteachsource.ascd.org/

For more information, send an e-mail to member@ascd.org; call 1-800-933-2723 or 703-578-9600; send a fax to 703-575-5400; or write to Information Services, ASCD, 1703 N. Beauregard St., Alexandria, VA 22311-1714 USA.

WHOLE CHILD
TENETS

1 **HEALTHY**
Each student enters school healthy and learns about and practices a healthy lifestyle.

2 **SAFE**
Each student learns in an environment that is physically and emotionally safe for students and adults.

3 **ENGAGED**
Each student is actively engaged in learning and is connected to the school and broader community.

4 **SUPPORTED**
Each student has access to personalized learning and is supported by qualified, caring adults.

5 **CHALLENGED**
Each student is challenged academically and prepared for success in college or further study and for employment and participation in a global environment.

THE WHOLE CHILD

The ASCD Whole Child approach is an effort to transition from a focus on narrowly defined academic achievement to one that promotes the long-term development and success of all children. Through this approach, ASCD supports educators, families, community members, and policymakers as they move from a vision about educating the whole child to sustainable, collaborative actions.

Designed to Learn relates to the **engaged**, **supported**, and **challenged** tenets. *For more about the ASCD Whole Child approach, visit* **www.ascd.org/wholechild.**